# MIXOLOGIST

## THE JOURNAL OF THE AMERICAN COCKTAIL

PUBLISHEI
Jared Brow

EDITOR
Anistatia Miller

MANAGING EDITOR
Robert Hess

REVIEW BOARD
Jared Brown, Dale DeGroff, Lowell Edmunds,
Robert Hess, David Wondrich

CONTRIBUTORS
Jared Brown, Paul Clarke, Lowell Edmunds, Phil Greene, Ted Haigh,
Robert Hess, Anistatia Miller, Darcy O'Neil, Gary Regan,
Audrey Saunders, David Wondrich

MIXELLANY
AN IMPRINT OF
JARED BROWN

# MIXOLOGIST
## THE JOURNAL OF THE AMERICAN COCKTAIL

COVER DESIGN
Ted Haigh

TEXT DESIGN
Anistatia Miller

*Mixologist: Journal of the American Cocktail* is published annually by Mixellany, an imprint of Jared Brown. A portion of net proceeds from the sales of *Mixologist* benefits the Museum of the American Cocktail, a non-profit 501(c) organization dedicated to the celebration of the American Cocktail's rich history.

All correspondence should be addressed to:
Jared Brown,
459 Columbus Avenue, Suite 201,
New York NY 10024 USA.

Email info@mixellany.com

ISBN: 0-9760937-0-7

# CONTENTS

## FROM THE EDITOR

**T**HE FIRST TIME IS ALWAYS the hardest. In the case of publishing this inaugural volume of *Mixologist: The Journal of the American Cocktail*, no truer words can sum up the days, weeks and months of sorting through the submissions from numerous cocktailians who've spent months and years delving into the origins of classic Cocktails, the history of famous spirits, the fact and fallacy of various techniques, and the future of Cocktails in a world that's clamoring for more creations.

Naturally, the idea for publishing this scholarly journal of all things relating to Cocktails was born—you guessed it—over Cocktails. At the second annual Southern Comfort Tales of the Cocktails gathering down in New Orleans, a group of us had convened for pre-dinner Sazeracs at Tujague's. And during the course of conversation, Robert Hess, Dave Wondrich and I discussed how it was time for Cocktails and the scholars who love them to have a forum for serious discussions about origins, about the people who created them, about the ingredients, about the business itself. These seeds of thought grew into what you see here.

We put out a call for entries with a ridiculously limited deadline—60 days—and hoped for the best. The review board, consisting of Jared Brown, Dale DeGroff, Lowell Edmunds, Hess and Wondrich sifted through manuscripts whose subjects ranged as far a field as an index of cordial and liqueur densities for use in layering drinks and the origins of the Cocktail shaker.

In the end, we decided that the *Mixologist's* first volume should focus on the history of classic cocktails. (Next year's volume will be primarily devoted to discussions on bar operations, bar ware, and organoleptic testing techniques for professionals and aficionados.) And we can assure you, each of the authors of this collection of never-before-published articles is an authority in his or her own right in the cocktailian world.

Thanks to all of our contributors—Gary Regan, Lowell Edmunds, David Wondrich, Audrey Saunders, Paul Clarke, Darcy O'Neil, Phil Greene, Robert Hess, and Ted Haigh—for making this volume a thought-provoking read for both novices and serious Cocktail scholars.

What would we have done without the patient and always insightful Managing Editor Robert Hess by our side throughout the entire process and the visual talent of Ted "Dr. Cocktail" Haigh, who took time to create *Mixologist's* first cover? Thank you, gentlemen, for all of your support and great work.

We want to take a moment to remind all of you that when you are down in New Orleans, take some time to visit the Museum of the American Cocktail and explore the 200-year-long visual history of the Cocktail or participant in one of the Museum's many seminars conducted throughout the year.

But for now, pour yourself your favorite libation, sit back and savor a new world of discovery which I hope you will find in these pages. Join us in celebrating one of America's most enduring icons, the Cocktail.

Anistatia Miller
Editor

# OUR CONTRIBUTORS

## PAUL CLARKE

Paul Clarke's interest in classic Cocktails was sparked by a cold Gimlet on a hot summer evening. He has a growing collection of vintage cocktail manuals, and is currently trying to track down every rye whiskey made in the United States. Paul works as an editor and freelance writer; his work has appeared in *E/The Environmental Magazine*, *Seattle* magazine and other regional publications. He lives in Seattle.

## LOWELL EDMUNDS

The critical success of Lowell Edmunds' *Martini, Straight Up: The Classic American Cocktail* (1998), a revised edition of *The Silver Bullet: The Martini in American Civilization* (1981) brought him into contact with the illuminati and glitterati of the drinks trade (and avocation) on both sides of the Atlantic. An Italian translation, with a preface by Umberto Eco, appeared in 2000. He has published "The Secular Sacrament," a memoir, in *Social History of Alcohol Review*; also "Women and Cocktails in Victorian America," in the same journal and a review-article. He has been a professor of Classics at Harvard, Boston College, Johns Hopkins and Rutgers; and a visiting professor at Princeton and, in Italy, at the Universities of Venice and Trent.

## PHIL GREENE

Attorney, author of the manuscript *Creole Gumbo*, and freelance historian, Phil Greene is a descendant of the Peychaud family of New Orleans and the Bordeaux region of France (home to Chateau Peychaud). Among Phil's ancestors was the illustrious Antoine Amedee Peychaud, the nineteenth-century New Orleans pharmacist who concocted Peychaud's Aromatic Cocktail Bitters and is credited with coining the term "Cocktail." As the story goes, Peychaud mixed a brandy and bitters (for their medicinal powers, of course) concoction, served in a double-ended, hourglass egg cup, called a *coquetier*, which later coined into the term "Cocktail." This brandy drink eventually evolved into the Sazerac, a New Orleans' signature drink, which is still made with Peychaud's Bitters. Phil has become an authority on the life of the ironically initialed A.A. Peychaud and the tale of the Cocktail tale, as well as New Orleans history, in general. A graduate of New Orleans' Loyola University School of Law, Phil is Senior Counsel for Internet Technology with the U.S. Department of Commerce and lives in Washington, DC with his wife and three daughters.

### TED HAIGH

By profession, Ted Haigh (aka: Dr. Cocktail) is a noted graphic designer for major Hollywood movies. His heart and soul, however, belong to the history of the American Cocktail. Previously the Cocktail & Spirits Maven for the America Online, he has developed, with Martin Doudoroff, cocktaildb.com, an encyclopedic database of drink recipes, ingredient definitions and bibliographic entries, which is acclaimed as a resource for writers, researchers, barmen and aficionados alike. His premises and theories of the Cocktail and its constituent components have been widely quoted in books, newspapers, magazines, and on the Web internationally. His new book, *Vintage Spirits & Forgotten Cocktails*, (Rockport Publishers) has just been released.

### ROBERT HESS

Robert Hess, Group Manager and Technical Evangelist at Microsoft, traces his interest in Cocktails to a childhood fascination of bartenders, who effortlessly transformed the contents of the bottles around them into gleaming jewels of refreshment. Eventually he took action on these early memories, absorbing all he could about the classic art of mixology. Using his culinary training as a canvas, he views Cocktails as a cuisine with the same artistic flavor potentials as that of any French chef. He has since become a ceaseless evangelist of quality Cocktails, working with restaurants, bartenders and consumers—as well as creating the informative and widely recognized website www.DrinkBoy.com—to increase recognition and respect for this undervalued art.

### ANISTATIA MILLER & JARED BROWN

Anistatia Miller and Jared Brown, authors and spirits specialists, drink and write about drinks for a living. Established in 1995, their web site *Shaken Not Stirred:® A Celebration of the Martini* (www.martini-place.com) led to the publication of the book by the same name (HarperCollins, 1997 and Europa Verlag, 1998). Their homage to the bubbly, *Champagne Cocktails*, was published two years later (Regan-Books, 1999). They are contributing Cocktail-, restaurant- and travel-editors for *Hamptons*, *Gotham*, *LA Confidential* and *Aspen Peak* magazines. Their articles have also appeared in *Wine Spectator*, *Cigar Aficionado*, *FoodArts*, *Wine & Dine* and *Northwest Palate*. They are also founders and co-publishers of the Museum of the American Cocktail's book and scholarly journal division.

Miller and Brown developed Heavy Water vodka's formula, which won the Beverage Tasting Institute's (BTI's) gold and "best of" designations in 2002. They also helped to develop gin, rum and vodka for America's first micro-distillery restaurant, The Bardenay. The gin received a BTI score of 92 points at its 2003 tasting.

They have devised proprietary Cocktail recipes for spirits companies including Kobrand, Bacardi and Remy Amérique, and have served as brand ambassadors for Martini & Rossi and Bacardi. This husband-and-wife team has made numerous national and local TV and radio appearances, discussing their favorite subjects—Cocktails and spirits. They've been quoted in *USA Today*, *The New York Times* and *Playboy*. And they've taken their show on the road, teaching professionals at the Vail ski resorts and consumers at Morton's Steakhouses nationwide, Southern Comfort's Annual Tales of the Cocktail Spirited Dinners as well as in private group classes.

## DARCY O'NEIL

Darcy S. O'Neil was born in Sarnia, Ontario and spent many of those years living near the beach. A cold Canadian beach, but a beach nonetheless. After high school, the decision of a career choice was whittled down to chemistry or the culinary arts. Chemistry won out because at the time it seemed logical that laboratory skills were more transferable to the kitchen than cooking skills to the lab. Four years of college later he received his diploma in chemistry.

After a six-year stint working in a world class oil and gas research facility, the time for change arrived, via a downsizing notice. After a couple of false starts in the pharmaceutical and information technology world's the possibility of going to chef school returned. During a period of quiet contemplation, and a few drinks, he was whacked with the epiphany stick and the marriage of chemistry and bartending dawned upon him.

With a little research into the world of mixology and a completely stocked home bar, that rivaled many bars and irritated his wife with all the clutter, the fusion of science and art began. As he rifled through the classic drinks to modern interpretations, and the occasional vile concoction, the chemistry skills started to refine the art. A whole new world of experimental flavors opened up in a way that satisfied his experimental curiosity and his culinary cravings. A bartender was born.

Currently, Darcy is employed as a bartender and is currently working on introducing people to great Cocktails.

### GARY REGAN

Gary and Mardee Regan are very highly regarded Cocktail connoisseurs, spirit experts, and authors, as well as bartending and restaurant consultants. Gary's latest, *The Joy of Mixology: The Consummate Guide to the Bartender's Craft*, has been called "a definitive and entertaining guide to the bartender trade" (*Publishers' Weekly*). They have also written for publications such as *Food & Wine, Playboy, Wine Spectator, Martha Stewart Living, All About Beer, Wine & Spirits, Cheers, FoodArts* and *Wine & Spirit International*. They consult for liquor companies and have lectured at The Smithsonian Institute, The Culinary Institute of America and The International Wine Center, New York.

### AUDREY SAUNDERS

Audrey Saunders joined the Carlyle in February, 2002 for the much-acclaimed reopening of New York's legendary Bemelman's Bar. Acknowledging that women and hard liquor are not generally associated with one another, Saunders' passion, which is evident in her work, goes beyond mixology. She skillfully takes Cocktails one step further, and at Bemelman's, a drink is not just a drink—it's a crafted masterpiece.

Early in her career, she attended night classes at the Institute of Culinary Education to expand her basic foundation for the blending of flavors and densities, for as most Michelin-starred chefs would agree, gastronomic perfection is found in the details. Though precise proportions and methods are less of a concern behind most bars, Saunders is a perfectionist and has been known to re-mix possible new recipes 40 or 50 times during the creation process before finally pinpointing the perfect components and measures for her recipes. Her menus at Bemelman's Bar, which change seasonally, feature truly unique Cocktails, including a number of her original creations as well as Old World classics.

Saunders' story behind the bar begins in 1996 when she was working concurrently in Brooklyn Heights and Manhattan at The Waterfront Ale House. The manager knew of her interest in Cocktail creation and suggested that she take a seminar at New York University that was being offered by Master Mixologist Dale DeGroff. After finishing the seminar, Saunders was so enthralled that she approached DeGroff, offering to work for free in exchange for training. By 1997, she became involved with DeGroff for special events for the Rainbow Room, such as an evening making drinks for the Mayor at Gracie Mansion.

In 1999, she and DeGroff opened Blackbird on East 49 Street where they spent a year working side by side, and Saunders painstakingly proved herself to regulars by mixing DeGroff's specialties to perfection. Since arriving at The Carlyle's Bemeleman's Bar, she has been sharing her time between New York and London. She spent the last two Thanksgiving holidays as a guest mixologist at The Ritz Hotel in London, where she worked closely with their staff. During her stays there, she also appeared on BBC prime-time television, BBC radio, and has also conducted cocktail seminars at Milk & Honey, UK. She has also been written about internationally, appearing in such publications as *The New York Times, The London Times, The Financial Times, BusinessWeek, The Wall Street Journal, Forbes, New York Magazine, Town & Country, Gentleman's Quarterly, Wine Enthusiast, Wine & Spirits*, and *InStyle* Magazine.

## DAVID WONDRICH

David Wondrich is an internationally-recognized authority on Cocktails and their history. He is a Contributing Editor at *Esquire* and writes for numerous other magazines on the subject, including *Saveur, Gotham, Wine and Spirits, Playboy* and *Drinks*. His first book, *Esquire Drinks: An Opinionated and Irreverent Guide to Drinking* (Hearst Books, 2002), has been acclaimed as "arguably the most enjoyable guide to entertaining with alcohol since Kingsley Amis's 1972 *On Drink*...brilliantly witty, irreverent and brimming with interesting trivia" David, who holds a Ph.D. in Comparative Literature from New York University, is also the motive force behind Slow Food's annual Tribute to Jerry Thomas, in which some of the nation's most respected mixologists get together to pay tribute to "Professor" Jerry Thomas (the man who wrote the first cocktail book, in 1862)—an event which *The New York Times* described as "an antiquarian lark, with overtones of a séance."

**BOTTLE DISPLAY STANDS**

**$11.00**

One of the many unique bar fixtures offered in the 1918 edition of the Albert Pick & Company saloon supplies catalog. (From the collection of Robert Hess.)

As any great chef or mixologist will tell you, it's the knowledge of the basics that creates the foundation for inspired
invention. In the Cocktail world, the search for the origins
of most classic drinks leads the seeker down a winding path
of veiled authorships, literary references, skewed timelines,
and numerous evolutions. Our inaurgural issue features the
results of years of scholarly research on the invention and
development of Punch, the Martini, the Gimlet, the Singapore Sling, the Bellini, and the Pina Colada conducted by
some of the world's best authorities in the field of...

# CLASSIC COCKTAILS

PLATE No. 12.

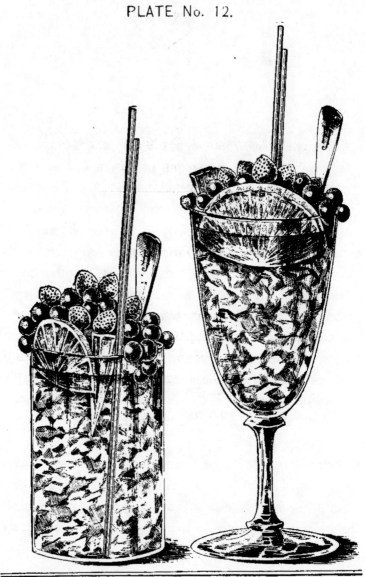

MISSISSIPPI PUNCH.     CURACOA PUNCH.

Punches enjoyed a two-century-long reign as the regent of Cocktails. By
the time these Punch presentations appeared in Harry Johnson's *New and
Improved Bartenders' Manual*, the Cocktail had replaced Punch as the
drink of choice among the masses. (From the collection of Dale DeGroff.)

# A BRIEF HISTORY OF PUNCH

BY DAVID WONDRICH

*Before the Cocktail became king, Punch was the favored social libation, combining spirits, citrus fruits, spices, sugar and water in a myriad of forms. David Wondrich traces Punch's curious origins and its evolution as it coursed through two centuries of popular culture. First appearing in a letter that dates back to 1632, Punch graced the lips of sailors and merchants involved in the East India trade. Bowls of Punch flowed at gatherings of nobles, sports enthusiasts, and literati during the British Empire's rise, throughout the American Revolution and well into Victoria's reign before it was supplanted by its down-the-hatch successor, the Cocktail.*

N 1862, JEREMIAH P. THOMAS, A NEW YORK bartender of some renown, published *How to Mix Drinks, or the Bon Vivant's Companion*, the world's first bartender's guide and the foundation-text for the fine art of mixing drinks.[1] The first section of the book is by far the largest, with 78 recipes. It's devoted not to the Cocktail, as one might expect, but to Punch. It's no accident that Punch gets pride of place. Although, judging by the twee, overfruited objects one finds usurping its name in contemporary lifestyle magazines, it has now fallen on very hard times indeed, it was once the sovereign ruler of the kingdom of mixed drinks. If, by the time Jerry Thomas got to it, Punch was nearing the end of its spectacular two-century reign, it still retained an aura of gentility no other mixed drink could approach. The first drink based on distilled spirits to gain widespread popularity and the one that brought citrus fruits into the mixologist's larder, Punch had made gentlemen accustomed to drinking liquor, and its concoction was one of the few culinary tasks one could perform without losing caste.

Amid the myriad of books that have been written about alcoholic beverages and their history, I've been unable to find a single one devoted to the long and curious history of Punch, and few indeed that give it more than a cursory glance, and so what follows must necessarily be speculative and woefully incomplete. Just about any history of beverage alcohol will tell you that the name "Punch" comes from the Hindi *panch* ("five") for the drink's standard number of ingredients (I'll get to them in a moment) and that Punch was an Indian notion, adopted by the various European merchants, freebooters and adventurers who

---

1. Jerry Thomas, *How to Mix Drinks, or the Bon Vivant's Companion* (New York: Dick & Fitzgerald, 1862).

found their way to the East in the seventeenth century.[2] During Punch's heyday this was the common wisdom about its origin, and it may very well be true. On the other hand, there are those who say "Punch" comes from "puncheon," a large cask in the 80 to 120 gallon range, from which India-bound English seafarers supposedly drew the spirits for their new drink. Although this seems less likely—in the inventory of the galleon *Leicester*, an early English East India-man specifically indicates that the small quantity of spirits carried was in "litle Barrells" or "runletts," small kegs in the 15 to 20 gallon range—it cannot be dismissed out of hand.[3]

It's safe to say, anyway, that the five ingredients—about which there was broad agreement—strongly suggest a non-European origin, since only one of them was common there and that was water. Everything else either came exclusively from the East or was much cheaper there and easier to come by (here I am merely repeating what Joseph Addison already observed three centuries ago). The citrus fruits—limes, lemons or citrons—which gave it its uniquely refreshing character were uncommon and expensive in the northern parts of Europe, where Punch enjoyed its greatest popularity, as was the cane sugar which balanced the drink's acidity. It got its kick from "arrack," a blanket term (derived from the Arabic word for "liquor") which was applied to a variety of Eastern distillates, none of them made from anything as ordinary as grapes, orchard fruits or malt.[4]

---

2. See, for a relatively early example, H. Porter and G. E. Roberts, *Cups and Their Customs*, (2nd Ed.) (London: John Van Voorst, 1869).

3. E.G.R. Taylor, ed., *The Troublesome Voyage of Captain Edward Fenton, 1582-83* (Cambridge: Hakluyt Society, 1959) pp. 133, 143.

4. Arrack came in three main kinds, "Goa arrack" or "Columbo arrack" was distilled in southern India and Ceylon from palm-sap, "Bengal arrack" in northern India from sugarcane, and "Batavia arrack" in the Dutch colony of that name—present-day Jakarta—and other parts of Indonesia and the Philippines, chiefly by the ethnic Chinese community. Originally this last was made exclusively from rice—when Antonio

The fifth ingredient, spices, was of course what caused the Europeans to set sail for the East in the first place. The particular ones which went into Punch could be as common as tea or nutmeg or as exotic as ambergris (basically, solidified whale cholesterol), but one could find none of them growing in the kitchen garden.[5] Yet since nobody competent in the languages and pre-colonial literature of the Indian Subcontinent seems to have yet delved into the matter of Punch, the exact genesis of Punch will have to remain an open question.

Wherever it was first concocted, this simple, versatile tipple (it was equally good hot or cold, as the climate demanded) proved particularly congenial to the English sailors and merchants involved in the East India trade. We know this from its first recorded appearance in the English language. This occurs in a 1632 letter found in the India Office records, in which one R. Adams writes to T. Colley, a merchant based at Petapoli on the Coromandel Coast (north of modern Madras, India): "I am very glad you have so good compani to be with all as Mr. Cartwright, I hop you will keep good house together and drincke punch by no allowanc."[6] (Note, besides the invented spelling, the healthy respect, even fear, which true Punch inspires in those who have—by some allowance—made its acquaintance.) We also know it by *palepunzen, bolleponge* and *pale bunze*, which are respectively the early Dutch, French and

---

Pigafetta, sailing with Magellan, encountered it in the Philippines, he pronounced it "stronger and better than that of palm." In fact, the relative weakness of Goa arrack was a common complaint; as one seventeenth-century traveler observed, "Bengal is much stronger than that of Goa," while even William Dampier, who preferred Goa ("it makes most delicate punch") conceded that "it must have a dash of Brandy to hearten it." At some point in the seventeenth century, the Batavia Chinese took a leaf from the Bengalis and began making their arrack from sugarcane, although they retained the traditional Chinese technique of jump-starting fermentation with little cakes of moldy red rice. Eventually, this would become the most popular of the kinds.

5. Ted Haigh has prepared a valuable but alas unpublished monograph on the use of ambergris in drinks.

6. Oxford English Dictionary, s.v. punch.

German words for "Punch"—each of them being nothing more than a loose phonetic transcription of the English "bowl o' Punch."[7]

Like curry, port and over-amplified rock 'n' roll, Punch became one of those foreign things which the English seize on as being peculiarly their own. With that as an excuse, we'll turn our backs on everyone else and focus on the English and those who inherited their culture (or had it otherwise imposed on them).

It took awhile for this novel way of splicing the main-brace to follow the seafarers home. In 1634, James Howell, minutely surveying the drinks of the world in one of his famous *Epistles*, did not know Punch.[8] By mid-century, though, it was discernable on the horizon. Under the January 16, 1662 entry, the aristocratic diarist John Evelyn recorded a visit he and the Duke of York made late one evening to "an East India vessel" moored at the London docks.[9] There they had "entertainment of several curiosities," including "Punch etc." The quick "etc" suggests that Punch at least was a known quantity not needing further explication. Perhaps, but it certainly wasn't yet an everyday sort of tipple. For one thing, it appears nowhere in the consummate document of the age, Samuel Pepys' diary. From 1659 to 1669, Pepys kept meticulous note of just about every drop of liquid to pass his lips, and that in itself was no small task. From spiced wine and buttered beer to brandy and "strong water [i.e., booze] made of juniper" (one of the earliest mentions of gin), Pepys pretty much drank

---

7. Henry Yule and A. C. Burnell, *Hobson Jobson: the Anglo-Indian Dictionary* (1886; Ware, Hertfordshire: Wordsworth, 1996) s.v. punch.

8. See his letter of August 2, 1630; *Familiar Letters or Epistolae Ho-elianae* (London: Temple Classics, 1903).

9. *The Diary of John Evelyn*, ed. John Bowle (Oxford: 1985).

10. There is a text-searchable edition of the diary available at www.gutenberg.net; see also Oscar A. Mendelsohn, *Drinking with Pepys* (London: MacMillan, 1963).

his way through the available list of beverages; if Punch had been in common use, he would've sniffed it out.[10]

Then there's Richard Head. In 1665, Head—perhaps early English prose fiction's most disreputable practitioner, and that's saying something—published the work for which he is remembered, *The English Rogue: Described in the Life of Meriton Latroon, A Witty Extravagant.* For "witty extravagant," read "complete and total dirtball." Latroon, the book's narrator, is a runaway apprentice who swipes, swills, swives and swindles his way through England and Ireland until the powers that be decide that the best place for him is anywhere else and transport him abroad. Head, an expert at swilling himself, renders his hero's in considerable detail. Nowhere in Britain does Latroon encounter Punch. Instead, he has to make do with things like "buttered sack"—hot sherry and butter—and "caudle"—hot spiced beer with eggs in it.[11]

In fact, other than the brandy used to fortify the sack,[12] rarely does he encounter strong waters at all. (On the other hand, when after a series of unfortunate and highly unlikely events Latroon ends up in Java, he not only drinks "very immoderately of punch" but marries the woman who supplies it to him. Nobody said he was stupid.) When, in his scurryvagation around the more unsavory parts of the British Isles, Latroon does come across spirits, they're drunk straight or as a "pop-in" to beer, and that only among very low society indeed. This needled beer, at least, appears to have been a lowlife favorite: see also Thomas Dekker's 1608 *The Bel-Man of London*, in which the senior member of the "ragged regiment of beggars" calls his crew to order

---

11. Ed. Michael Shinagel (Boston: New Frontiers, 1961). *The English Rogue* was continued by Francis Kirkman; his Volume II from 1671, set partly in India, has aq description of Punch made with "amber-grease"

12. Sack, from the Spanish *sacado*, "reserved," was simply young, sweet Spanish wine with a little grape distillate tipped in to prevent spoilage.

13. *The Guls Hornbook and The Belman of London* (London: Temple Classics, 1941).

while swigging from "a double Jug of Ale (that had the spirit of Aqua vitae in it, it smelt so strong)."[13]

Beyond this, an admittedly unsystematic survey of the literature of dissipation fails to turn up any other popular mixed drink involving distilled spirits. If the fifteenth and sixteenth centuries had seen strong waters breach the always-permeable boundary between the pharmaceutical drug and the recreational one and their production consequently spread to all corners of Europe, the ways in which they were consumed still owed more to the apothecary than the epicure. When they were consumed, it was generally straight, in drams.[14]

Once Punch made its presence known, it didn't take long for it to trickle deep into the bedrock of English social life. The turning point in its fortunes appears to have come in the 1670s. The opening year of the decade saw the first printed recipe for Punch appear in Hannah Wooley's pioneering cookbook, *The Queen-Like Closet, or Rich Cabinet*. Five years later it still had not penetrated to all corners of the Kingdom: when Henry Teonge, a Warwickshire parson encountered it aboard the HMS *Assistance*, which he was newly joining as ship's chaplain, he pronounced it "a liquor very strange to me" (it didn't remain that way for long, seeing as it flowed "like ditchwater" on board, with Teonge and the other officers going through several bowls of it a day).[15] By 1680, though, it had arrived, for in that year the rakish and well-connected Captain Alexander Radcliffe published his "Bacchanalia Coelestia," subtitled "A Poem in Praise of Punch," and if Radcliffe knew it, the King knew it, and if the King knew it, everyone did.[16]

---

14. R.J. Forbes' invaluable *A Short History of Distillation* (Leiden: E.J. Brill, 1948) has some useful material on early consumption of spirits.

15. *The Diary of Henry Teonge*, ed. G.E. Mainwaring (New York: Harper & Bros., 1927); see, *inter alia*, June 1, 1675, July 10, 1675 and May 9, 1978.

16. London, 1680.

After that, things move fast. In 1684, we find Punch deep in the wilds of Yorkshire, where George Meriton includes it in the verses he writes in praise of Yorkshire ale.[17] In 1694, it's Admiral Edward Russell, the hero of La Hogue (where he had trounced the French fleet), filling a Spanish fountain with Punch for six thousand—it took five pounds of nutmeg just to spice it and a boy in a rowboat to ladle it out.[18] Six years later, pulp fictioneer Ned Ward could opine in prose that Punch "if composed of good ingredients, and prepared with true judgement, exceeds all the simple [i.e., straight, unmixed], potable products in the universe" and in verse that "Had our forefathers but thy virtues known, / Their foggy ale to lubbers they'd have thrown."[19] The Age of Punch had arrived. As long as there were lubbers—bumpkins—to keep ale alive its triumph was not complete, but Punch did cast many of the other traditional compound drinks of Olde Englande, turbid, egg-rich things based on ale and wine, into the outer darkness where is wailing and gnashing of teeth. The seal on its progress was its adoption, in the early part of the new century, by the Whigs—the liberal element in English politics—as their unofficial party drink (in both senses of the phrase). The Tories, reactionaries, stuck to port for a time, but eventually they too yielded to the attraction of the "flowing bowl" (a phrase which was already proverbial when Matthew Prior used it in one of his poems in 1718).[20]

Of course, drinks don't generally reach eminent positions like the one Punch now occupied without making

---

17. *The Praise of York-shire Ale* (York, 1685; rpt. York: Rusholmes, 1975).

18. This widely-repeated story, like so many associated with strong drink, has been maddeningly difficult to track to its origins. The earliest iteration I have been able to find is in Robert Chambers' *Chambers' Book of Days* (London: R & K Chambers, 1864), under October 25th.

19. *The London Spy*, ed. Paul Hyland (1700; 4th ed. 1709; East Lansing: Colleagues, 1993).

20. *Solomon on the Vanity of the World*, II, 106. In *Poems on Several Occasions*, ed. A. R. Waller (Cambridge: 1905).

some compromises. For one thing, folks soon discovered that its five-part formula was rather like a five-legged table; it could lose a leg and still stand foursquare. Take, for example, the 1694 order put out by the English government of Bombay: "if any man comes into a victualling house to drink Punch, he may demand one quart good Goa *arak*, half a pound of sugar, and half a pint of good lime water, and make his own Punch."[21] No nutmeg, no tea, no ambergris. Not that spice exactly disappeared from Punch recipes, but let's just say that nobody was about to call off a perfectly good Punch party for want of a blade of mace or what-have-you.

Then there was the question of the arrack. "Rack," as it was commonly known, was a funky, usually fiery and always expensive distillate (the long and arduous journey it had to make around the Cape of Good Hope meant that it would never be cheap). It was a taste which needed acquiring. Some never did—"I don't love rack Punch," as Jonathan Swift wrote to his beloved Stella in 1711, "I love it better with brandy; are you of my opinion?"[22] History is silent as to her reply. Many others, anyway, were not of his opinion. In his popular 1730 farce, *The Tragedy of Tragedies, or the Life and Death of Tom Thumb the Great*, Henry Fielding has King Arthur issue one of the great royal decrees in literature:

"To-day it is our Pleasure to be drunk, / And this our Queen shall be as drunk as we." While his Queen is nothing loth in theory, she does have her scruples:
If the capacious Goblet overflow
With *Arrack-Punch*—'fore George! I'll see it out;

---

21. Hobson Jobson, loc. cit.
22. *Journal to Stella* (London: Dent, n.d.); the entry is from Nov. 18.

Of *Rum,* or *Brandy,* I'll not taste a Drop.

The King answers with the magnanimity that is the sign of true-bred royalty:

> Tho' *Rack,* in *Punch,* Eight Shillings be a Quart,
>     And *Rum* and *Brandy* be no more than Six,
> Rather than quarrel, you shall have your Will
> (II, i).[23]

These were in fact the prevailing prices at the time, although the next year James Ashley began selling arrack Punch for only six shillings and Brandy or Rum Punch for four at his "Sign of the Two Punch Bowls" in Ludgate Hill, only steps from St. Paul's Cathedral.[24] Ashley made a killing. He lived until 1776, prosperous and successful to the last (six shillings was still a lot of money—about one one-hundredth of a year's living wage). In any case, whether it was price or taste driving the substitution, arrack was displaced often and early—Hannah Wooley's Punch calls for a mixture of brandy and wine, as does Captain Radcliffe's, and late-seventeenth century references to Rum Punch abound, especially in the American colonies—without appearing to have caused undue suffering in the populace.

Be it filled with arrack from the East Indies, rum from the West Indies or brandy from right across the Channel, throughout the Age of Enlightenment and the Napoleonic Age which followed, and a good part of the Victorian one to boot, anybody with any pretense to flash or style took communion from the punchbowl. Punch wasn't solely the province of aristocratic rakehells, highwaymen and Regency bucks, though; even a small-town shopkeeper such as

---

23. In *British Dramatists from Dryden to Sheridan*, ed George H. Nettleton, et al. (Carbondale: Southern Illinois UP, 1969).

24. Quoted in David Peabody, "The London Coffee House," www.freemasonrytoday.com/coffee.

Thomas Turner, who kept a meticulous diary in the 1760s, would occasionally indulge in "an agreeable bowl of punch" (it helped that he was friends with the local officer of excise, who would contribute confiscated bottles of smuggled brandy to the cause).[25] For a time in the early Victorian years, the Royal Navy even decreed that, for ships on foreign station, the official grog ration—each man was entitled to four or five ounces a day of 109° proof rum, mixed with two parts water—had to have lemon juice and sugar added to it, and if that doesn't yield Punch I don't know what does.[26] But if Punch was down there among the shopkeepers and scurvy-prone sailors, it wasn't entirely of them. Though the Thomas Turners of the world handled it, it was the Charles Morrises who owned it.

From the last years of the old century until 1831, when he resigned his post at age 86, Captain Charles Morris was the spirit presiding over the venerable and riotous London institution known as the "Sublime Society of Beef Steaks." At five o'clock every Saturday from November to June, 24 aristocratic sports and their guests gathered together to eat nothing but grilled steak (with a few fixings) and drink nothing but port wine and Arrack Punch.[27] (In 1785, when George Augustus Frederick, the Prince of Wales, wanted in they couldn't very well put him on a waiting list so they had to make him the twenty-fifth member). Morris, who had an extraordinary facility for throwing together impromptu verses and songs, many of them quite filthy, was sort of a song-leader and, more to the point, the man in charge of making the Punch. "It was amusing

25. *The Diary of Thomas Turner*, 1754-1765, ed. David Vaisey (Oxford: 1984); see especially Dec. 24, 1764.

26. James Pack, *Nelson's Blood: the Story of Naval Rum* (Annapolis: Naval Institute P, 1996).

27. This was the ultimate origin of the ancient New York institution, the "Beefsteak"—a supper where a group of politically-connected gents would sit around eating beef with their hands and washing it down with beer.

to see him at his laboratory at the sideboard," one initiate later recalled, "stocked with the various products that enter into the composition of that nectareous mixture: then smacking an elementary glass or two, and giving a significant nod, the fiat of its excellence." Alas, if Morris' exact recipe survives, I have not been able to find it; all I have are tantalizing descriptions of the "mantling beauties" of this "potent" and "fascinating draught 'That flames and dances in its crystal bound'" (the quote is from Milton, who alas did not know Punch).[28]

It's safe to say, however, that Morris' version of Arrack Punch would've had little in common with the one that Mr. Colley was supposed to steer clear of in Petapoli. By the by, the early 1800s, Englishmen were in a mood to experiment, and Punch could include everything from milk and brown stout to orange-flower water and *capillaire*, a French syrup infused with maidenhair fern (the Prince Regent's favorite Punch, of which he drank widely and deep, called for ten ingredients; others used still more). At least the Steaks' arrack would've been genuine, which was not always the case—London's Vauxhall Gardens was famous for serving an Arrack Punch in which the "arrack" was in fact nothing more than cheap rum flavored with benzoin, a kind of tree-gum. As Thackeray notes in *Vanity Fair*, a work in which Vauxhall's Rack Punch plays a brief but pivotal role, "there is no headache in the world like that caused by Vauxhall Punch."[29] Thus speaketh experience.

In Thackeray's day, though, worse things than imitation arrack were finding their way into the flowing bowl. Whisky, for one. For much of its history, rough, smoky, clear distillate of high proof and little finesse, the unaged uisce beatha that was being illicitly distilled throughout the glens

---

28. John Timbs, *Clubs and Club Life in London* (London: Chatto & Windus, 1886).

29. See Chapter VI, "Vauxhall."

and moors of Scotland and Ireland was strictly off-limits to the genteel drinker. A rare exception was Captain Edmund Burt, an English engineer who spent most of the 1730s in the Scottish Highlands. Normally, he traveled with a bottle of his own brandy (and, of course, lemons and sugar) to avoid tasting the stuff. But even the stoutest oak must yield to a gale, and one evening found him in a hut with nothing to drink but river-water or the whisky a parcel of smugglers was transporting down from the glens. Luckily, he still had a few lemons, with which he "so far qualified the ill taste of the spirit as to make it tolerable." It was not an experiment he repeated. As for everyone else in "North Britain " (as Scotland was supposed to be called then), if we can trust Burt half of them didn't know Punch and the other half didn't like it. It would be hard to come up with a better spokesman for the ignorant ones than the landlord in the hills outside of Inverness who quite seriously asked the Captain's servant, squeezing lemons for his master's Punch, "if those were apples he was squeezing." In Inverness, on the other hand, where lemons "are seldom wanting" and "Punch is very reasonable...few care to drink it, as thinking the claret a much better liquor" (French wines were plentiful and cheap in the more urbanized parts of the country).[30]

But then came the '45, when Scotland rose up and got slapped down again, and the clearance of the Highlands, and the British—okay, English—military roads and a whole lot of other civilization, and next thing you know the Scots and the Irish are hitting the Punch. In fact, it's something of a national beverage. Most of the formula is perfectly orthodox: hot water, sugar and whisky. But only on the rare occasions when the Punch is made cold does the juice of the lemon enter into it; otherwise, it is, as one

---

30. *Burt's Letters from the North of Scotland*, ed. Andrew Simmons (1876; Edinburgh: Burlinn, 1998); see particularly Letters VII, XVII and XVIII.

authority maintains, "deleterious and must be eschewed," and only the peel is used. This authority, one R. Shelton MacKenzie, the editor of the *Noctes Ambrosianae* (an interminable series of fictional dialogues between various Scottish intellectuals who drink Punch at Ambrose's tavern in Edinburgh and ruminate the issues of the day), goes on to note (with clearer ethnography than grammar), "In the rural parts of Scotland, at the harvest-home, I have seen the Punch made in small wooden tubs which, as made to hold the fourth part of a boll of corn, is called a *firlot* [i.e., about ten gallons]. The quantity of this Punch those men can and do drink in Scotland is wonderfully large." Seeing as the mixture was traditionally two parts water to one part strong whisky, it's difficult to see how any harvesting would get done at all.[31]

Eventually, this hot Whisky Punch, alias "Hot Toddy," would spread south of the Tweed and across the Atlantic and to every corner of the earth where a lousy climate and poor heating make a warming drink an object of utility. This includes Ireland—unless in fact it had spread from Ireland to Scotland in the first place. In any case, it became associated closely enough with the Irish as to become an instrument of satire, as in Samuel Ferguson's 1838 *Father Tom and the Pope, or A Night at the Vatican*, a disreputable but quite amusing poke at the Irish clergy (Ferguson himself was Irish). When Father Tom from County Leitrim finds himself in "Room," you see, the Pope "axed him to take pot look wid him." It doesn't take long for the Holy Father to break out the wine, whereupon Father Tom produces a bottle of good *putteen* (bootleg Irish whiskey) from

30. John Wilson et al., *Noctes Ambrosianae*, ed. R. Shelton MacKenzie, five vols (New York: Redfiels, 1854), January, 1828.

32. Philadelphia: Peterson, 1879; this edition wrongly attributes the work to John Fisher Murray.

under his cassock and instructs the Pope how to make Punch: "Put in the sperits first…and then put in the sugar; and remember, every dhrop ov wather you put in after that, spoils the Punch."[32] Note the absence of lemon of any kind, be it peel, pulp, pip or juice. The fact that such a concoction, formally indistinguishable from Hot Toddy or Hot Sling, can be called "Punch" is a sign that the word is losing its specificity, like "Martini" has in our day (imagine what Humphrey Bogart would've said if someone had offered him a "Chocolate Martini").

Meanwhile, in England things were changing, too. Whisky wasn't the worst of it. To find how truly low Punch had sunk, you would've had to go to a place like Limmer's Hotel, a London "resort for the sporting world…where you heard nothing but the language of the turf, and where men with not very clean hands used to make up their books," as Captain Gronow, the one-man archive of Regency gossip, later recalled.[33] Evidently the bookies rather set the tone for Limmer's standards of hygiene: according to Gronow, it was "the most dirty hotel in London." No matter; the clientele was frighteningly aristocratic and couldn't care less about such bourgeois values as cleanliness or comfort (a commodity in which Limmer's was also lacking). As long as the action was hot and the establishment kept the nouveaux riches and tradesmen out, it could count on their patronage. Particularly if John Collins (yes, *that* John Collins), the hotel's headwaiter, was at hand to fetch a brimming glass of its famous Punch, which was based not on arrack, rum or brandy (the three canonical Punch spirits), nor on whisky, but on "blue ruin"—gin.

---

33. *Reminiscences of Captain Gronow* (London: Smith, Elder, 1862), cap. "London Hotels in 1814."

Now, "Gin Punch" is a phrase which would've struck Jonathan Swift and his contemporaries not unlike the way "Malt Liquor Martini" strikes us today. Gin was not genteel—and if by the early nineteenth century it was no longer the liquid crack it had been in Swift's day, it was still nobody's idea of a classy tipple. Yet the highest reaches of society often find ways to come together with the lowest, and Regency London was no exception. Slumming in low-class "gin palaces" was a popular diversion for the "Fancy"—those fashionable young sparks who devoted their leisure hours to cultivating pugilists and jockeys and betting on the results of their proteges' labors. The tastes they acquired in establishments like the "sluicery" the aristocratic Corinthian Tom takes his equally well-bred friend Jerry Hawthorne to in *Life in London*, Pierce Egan's 1821 sporting-life classic—a nasty dive populated by broken-down old whores, street urchins and gin-soaked beggars—followed them to their more characteristic haunts, the Club, the Hotel, the Officers' Mess.[34] Even though some continued to agree with the young dandy caricatured in the *New Monthly Magazine* in 1828 that Gin Punch was "Vastly vulgar, by Petersham—only fit for the Cider-cellar,"[35] others did not—Lord Byron, for one, who (if his mistress is to be believed) wrote the last *Cantos of Don Juan* "with repeated glasses of Gin Punch at his side."[36]

The precise formula for Limmer's Gin Punch is probably lost forever. If it was anything like the Gin Punch the Garrick Club—another place where the bluebloods

---

34. New York: Appleton, 1904; Book II, cap. ii.
35. Reprinted in *The Mirror of Literature, Amusement, and Instruction*, October 11, 1828. Petersham was a famous dandy (he dressed only in brown and had a vast collection of snuff-boxes); the Cider Cellars was a vastly rowdy hole-in-the-wall in Covent Garden where the social elite went to get tanked and sing obscene songs. It is of course mentioned in Egan.
36. *Brooklyn Eagle*, Nov. 4, 1885.

and the sports rubbed up against each other—was dishing out at the time, it would've been a simple concoction of gin, lemon juice, sugar (or maraschino liqueur, as the Garrick Club's used) and soda water.[37] The presence of this last ingredient would mean that it had to be made in smaller batches than the Rack Punch of old, and indeed the Garrick Club's recipe makes only a relatively modest three pints. This seems like a trivial point, but in fact it's an indicator of a tectonic change in the world of mixed drinks. Gin Punch was Punch's last turn in the limelight. The drinks which were beginning to replace it at the cutting edge of mixological chicness were served by the glass, not the bowl and came from America, not India.

For two centuries, the fortunes of Punch in British America had been like those at home, only more so. Punch was adopted pretty much instantly by the Colonists—as early as 1684, we find one Thomas Tryon fulminating against a "pernicious sort of Drink in great Reputation and Use amongst [the colonists], call'd, *PUNCH*."[38] Pernicious or not, its distribution seems to have been universal, both geographically and socially: if we find the aristocratic Colonel William Byrd drinking Rack Punch with backcountry gentlemen on his 1728 mission to determine the Virginia-Carolina border,[39] we also find rum Punch present in its plenty at the clandestine meetings a group of African slaves held to plan the abortive uprising that would be known as the New York Conspiracy of 1741.[40] To cite more examples would be superfluous—everyone drank Punch who could get their hands on it, and most people could.

---

37. Timbs, op. cit.
38. *The Planters Speech to His Countrymen* (London: 1684).
39. William Byrd's *Histories of the Dividing Line betwixt Virginia and North Carolina*, ed. William K. Boyd (1929; New York: Dover, 1967).
40. See the trial testimony collected in 1744 by Daniel Horsmanden and reprinted as *The New York Conspiracy*, ed. Thomas J. Davis (Boston: Beacon, 1971).

After the Revolution, though, American drinking habits began going their own way. Nothing shows this more clearly than a glance at Jerry Thomas' book in comparison with some roughly contemporaneous English ones: *Drinking Cups and their Customs*, by H. Porter and G. E. Roberts,[41] William Terrington's *Cooling Cups and Dainty Drinks* [42] and Richard Cook's *Oxford Night Caps, a Collection of Receipts for Making Various Beverages Used in the University*.[43] Focusing only on the sections dealing with Punch, between them, these three books contain 77 recipes for Punch—one less than Thomas'. Of these, all but three are for multiple servings. The Punches in Thomas' book differ only slightly in kind. A handful might call for uniquely American ingredients such as Monongahela whiskey or Catawba wine, but the vast majority are virtually indistinguishable from their Transatlantic analogues, in all but one respect: of Thomas' 78 Punch recipes, 19—practically 25 percent—are for single servings.

This may not seem like such a big deal, and yet one may announce a revolution in small type as well as large, and this was indeed a revolution, one which Punch would only survive at the cost of its throne and its fortune. True, there had always been such a thing as a "sneaker" of Punch, a kind of large cup or small bowl which provided a (large) individual serving, and as far back as 1731, James Ashley was offering to make a quantity as small as a "half-quartern" (2 ounces) of arrack, rum or brandy into punch, which would be difficult to get more than one drink out of (especially considering how Anglo-Saxons put the stuff away).[44] But by and large, in the English and Colonial American

---

42. 41. See Note 2.
42. London: Routledge, n.d. [1869].
43. "New edition, enlarged" (Oxford: Slatter & Rose, 1871). If this has been enlarged from the first edition of 1827, it is only slightly, as they are nearly the same in length.
44. See Note 21.

tradition (and the Continental European tradition, for that matter), Punch had always been a convivial beverage, meant to be shared among a group of like-minded tipplers.

The ritual of the Punch bowl was a secular communion, welding a group of good fellows together into a temporary sodality whose values superseded all others— or, in plain English, a group of men gathered around a bowl of Punch could be pretty much counted on to see it to the end, come what may. This was all in good fun, but it required its participants to have a large block of uncommitted time on their hands. As the nineteenth century wore on, this was less and less likely to be the case. Industrialization and improved communications and the rise of the bourgeoisie all made claims on the individual that militated against partaking of the flowing bowl. Not that the Victorians were exactly sober, by our standards, but neither could they be as wet as their forefathers. As Robert Chambers put it in 1864, "Advanced ideas on the question of temperance have, doubtless, ...had their influence in rendering obsolete, in a great measure, this beverage."[45]

This isn't the only reason Punch fell by the wayside, of course. Improvements in distilling and, above all, aging of liquors meant that they required less intervention to make them palatable. The rise of a global economy made for greater choice of potables and a more fragmented culture of drink. Central heating to some degree dimmed the charms of hot Punch. Ideas of democracy and individualism extended to men's behavior in the bar-room, where they were less likely to all settle for the same thing or let someone else choose what they were to drink. Like all social institutions, the Bowl of Punch was subject to a plethora of subtle and incremental strains. Eventually, by mid-century, they toppled it, with most of the pull

---

45. Chambers, loc. cit. (see Note 16).

coming from America. Punch was out and the Cocktail, the down-the-hatch, out-the-door-and-back-to-work drink par excellence, was in.

Punch didn't disappear, of course. Like other survivors, it adapted to the prevailing reality and carved out whatever niche for itself it could. The Whisky Sour, the Daiquiri, the Sidecar and even the Margarita and the Cosmopolitan are, essentially, Punches cut to Cocktail shape. And then there are those things you find in the food magazines. ...

*Note: This is an enlarged version of an article that first appeared in* The Snail, *the newsletter of the Slow Food America organization.*

# THE RISE AND FALL OF THE MARTINI

## FOLLOWING THE COURSE OF THE MARTINI THROUGHOUT HISTORY

BY ROBERT HESS

*Few Cocktails have stirred the emotions of drinks scholars the world over as the Martini. Debates—both written and oral—have raged over the Silver Bullet's authoriship, evolution and its execution for over a century. Robert Hess surveys his personal view of the drink's evolution through his extensive research of the historical records and offers readers an opportunity to launch into their own journey of self-discovery through a structured tasting flight. For what is any Cocktail worth if it doesn't refresh and satisfy on a purely subjective level?*

# THE SCHIZOID COCKTAIL

THERE IS PERHAPS NO OTHER COCKTAIL that is better known, or less understood, then the Martini. Talk with any patron at the bar about what a Martini is, and most likely you will receive a variety of responses—and sometimes a fight. The confusion is not helped any by cocktail lounges that proudly display their "Martini menus" which list off dozens of different "Martinis" that their bartenders will happily mix up for you. With such cocktails as the Cosmopolitan, Lemon Drop and Manhattan all being categorized as types of Martinis, it is no wonder that many patrons of the bar find it easier to order a Bud Light than try to figure out what a Martini really is.

As you look into the origins and evolution of the Martini, you soon see that it has suffered a sort of schizophrenia all of its life. Not only has its recipe been in a constant state of flux, even its name has been the source of serious confusion.

## MARTINI ORIGINS

Looking through the historical record, it becomes apparent that the Martini evolved—either directly or indirectly—out of a slightly older cocktail, the Martinez. In his 1884 book, *Modern Bartender's Guide*, O.H. Byron was the first to list the Martinez Cocktail, but simply says it is the same as a Manhattan, only made with gin. Jerry Thomas then listed this recipe in the 1887 edition of his book, *The Bar-Tender's Guide*, which is quite similar to the recipe for the Manhattan that he lists earlier in the same book—except of course the substitution of Old Tom gin for the rye whiskey:

### MARTINEZ COCKTAIL.
(Use small bar-glass)

Take:
1 dash of Boker's bitters.
2 dashes of Maraschino.
1 pony of Old Tom gin.
1 wine-glass of Vermouth.
2 small lumps of ice.
Shake up thoroughly, and strain into a large cocktail glass. Put a quarter of a slice of lemon in the glass and serve. If the guest prefers it very sweet, add two dashes of gum syrup.[1]

Several of the often-quoted, but equally contradictory, stories regarding the origin of the Martini, start with the Martinez, and use that as the foundation for the name. It isn't until 1888 that we first find a Cocktail going specifically by the name of Martini in Harry Johnson's *New and Improved Bartenders' Manual*:

### MARTINI COCKTAIL.
(Use a large bar glass)

Fill the glass up with ice;
2 or 3 dashes of Gum Syrup
2 or 3 dashes of bitters (Boker's genuine only);
1 dash of curaçao;
one-half wine glassful of Old Tom Gin;
one-half wine glassful of Vermouth.
Stir up well with a spoon, strain it into a fancy cocktail glass, squeeze a piece of lemon peel on top, and serve.
(see *illustration, plate No. 13*).[2]

---

1. Jerry Thomas, *The Bar-Tender's Guide* (New York: Dick & Fitzgerald,1887), p. 25.
2. Harry Johnson, *The New And Improved Illustrated Bartenders' Manual* (New York: Harry Johnson, 1888), p. 165.

A recipe that while not precisely the same as what we've seen earlier as a Martinez, it is indeed close. Recipes similar to the above appeared in several other books during this period, sometimes listed as Martinez, sometimes as Martini, and—at least in the case of the illustration in Harry Johnson's book—a Martine as well.

Before we leave these recipes behind, we might take a slightly closer look at them to gain an even better understanding of the form these Cocktails originally took. You might feel a little confused by these recipes when you see bitters, maraschino, curaçao and gum syrup being listed as possible ingredients. But at least you still see the gin and vermouth as you might expect. Don't get too comfortable yet, however. Even these two ingredients probably aren't what you would've thought.

Old Tom gin was the common gin used in cocktails in those days. It is no longer available, and was slightly different from the London Dry gin we have today. Old Tom was slightly sweetened as was the style in the 1700s. This was done in an effort to help mask some of the impurities found in the final product. By the mid-1800s, the distillation methods had become refined enough that this sweetening was no longer needed, and eventually we saw an unsweetened gin—dry gin—become popular. (*See Anistatia Miller's article on gin in this volume.*)

The vermouth listed in these recipes is also hiding its true nature from you. While today such a reference would be assumed to mean French—or dry—vermouth, such has not always been the case. It was the Italian—or sweet—vermouth that was first used as a Cocktail ingredient. And if only vermouth, with no qualifier, was listed as an ingredient, it could generally be assumed that it meant Italian. So the gin was sweet, the vermouth was sweet and

PLATE No. 13.

Danziger Goldwasse,

Yolk of a fresh cold **Egg**.

Chartreuse (yellow).

GOLDEN SLIPPER.

MARTINE COCKTAIL.

The Martini's predecessor, the Martine Cocktail, was presented in both on-the-rocks and straight-up versions in Harry Johnson's *New and Improved Bartenders' Manual*. (From the collection of Dale DeGroff.)

therefore it shouldn't be too much of a surprise to see a cherry sometimes listed as an appropriate garnish.

There are still a few surprises to see in these older recipes. Take a look at the quantity of ingredients being used. Jerry Thomas listed a "pony" of gin, and a "wine-glass" of vermouth, while Harry Johnson listed a half wine-glass of each in his version. In these recipes, a wine-glass is not what you think; otherwise these would be fairly stiff drinks indeed. It is generally accepted that the term "wine-glass," when used as a measurement, indicated approximately two fluid ounces. And a pony measured one ounce, just as it does today. Still, in each of these recipes, we see that the ratio of gin to vermouth is very much different from what you would ever imagine being served today, even to the point of using more vermouth than gin!

## HOW DRY I AM

It was in the early years of the 1900s that we begin seeing the Martini recipe evolve closer to what it is today. Several books listed the ingredients as gin, sweet vermouth and orange bitters, thus making it a simplified Martinez, such as George J. Kappeler's and Jacques Straub's versions:

### MARTINI COCKTAIL.

Half a mixing-glass full fine ice, three dashes orange bitters, one-half jigger Tom gin, one-half jigger Italian vermouth, a piece lemon-peel. Mix, strain into cocktail-glass. Add a maraschino cherry, if desired by customer.[3]

---

3. George J. Kappeler, *Modern American Drinks* (New York: Merriam Company, 1895), p. 38.

### MARTINI COCKTAIL
one-third jigger Italian vermouth.
two-thirds jigger gin.
I dash orange bitters. Stir well and serve.[4]

While these two recipes are 20 years apart in publication, they provide nearly identical recipes for the drink that is now almost universally referred to as a Martini. This appears to indicate that what a Martini was had finally been settled, and had been broadly accepted by both the drinking public and by the bartenders that served them. It is also during this same period that London Dry gin, as well as the French (dry) vermouth began to take hold. But what is a customer to do if he or she preferred this newer gin and vermouth used in their cocktail? Why they'd ask for a "Dry Martini," of course.

To accommodate, and encourage this new variation of the Martini, several books of the day included a recipe for a Dry Martini as well. French Cocktail researcher, Fernando Castellon recently uncovered what perhaps the first printed occurrence is of the "Dry Martini" in *American Bar—Boissons Anglaise & Américaines*, published in 1904. It provides the recipe as:

### DRY MARTINI COCKTAIL
Verre No. 5
Prendre le verre à mélange no. I, mettre quelques
morceaux de glace:
3 traits d'angostura ou orange bitter.
Finir avec gin et vermouth sec, quantités égales, remuer, passer
dans le verre no. 5, server avec un zeste de citron, une cerise ou
une olive, au gout du consommateur.

Which translates into English as:

---

4. Jacques Straub, *Drinks* (Chicago: The Hotel Monthly Press, 1914), p. 31.

### DRY MARTINI COCKTAIL
Glass No 5
Using mixing glass No 1, and a few pieces of ice:
3 dashes of angostura or orange bitter.
Finish with gin and dry vermouth, equal quantities, stir well, pour
into glass No 5, serve with a piece of lemon peel, a cherry or an
olive, based on the taste of the consumer.

To accommodate, and encourage this new variation
of the Martini, several books of the day included a recipe
for a Dry Martini as well. Here is the one from the 1914
edition of the book *Drinks* by Jacques Straub:

### DRY MARTINI COCKTAIL
one-half jigger French vermouth.
one-half jigger dry gin. Stir.[5]

And then from 1925, here is another pair of recipes from a book
published in Boston (Note that this was during Prohibition):

### MARTINI COCKTAIL.
Three dashes orange bitters; two-thirds Tom gin; one-third Italian
vermouth; small piece of lemon peel. Fill with ice, mix, and strain
into a cocktail glass.[6]

### MARTINI COCKTAIL—DRY.
Two dashes orange bitters; two-thirds dry gin; one-third French
vermouth; small piece lemon peel. Fill with ice, mix, and strain into
a cocktail glass.[7]

We see a little confusion enter into the picture in
1930, when *The Savoy Cocktail Book* was published in London. Author Harry Craddock listed two different recipes
for a Dry Martini. The first is under the title "Dry Mar-

---

5. Jacques Straub, *Drinks* (Chicago: The Hotel Monthly Press, 1914), p. 31.
6. *The Cocktail Book: A Sideboard Manual for Gentlemen* (Boston: St. Botolph
Society, 1925), p. 21.
7. Ibid.

tini Cocktail" (in the "D" section of the book), only to be accompanied later on with a recipe for a "Martini (dry) Cocktail" (in the "M" section of the book).

### DRY MARTINI COCKTAIL.
one-half French Vermouth.
one-half Gin.
I dash Orange Bitters.
Shake well and strain into cocktail glass.[8]

### MARTINI (DRY) COCKTAIL.
one-third French Vermouth.
two-thirds Dry Gin.
Shake well and strain into cocktail glass.[9]

The fact that in this one book we see two different recipes for a cocktail going by the name of Dry Martini perhaps foreshadows some of the debate that in later years existed as to how to properly make this legendary Cocktail.

It is important to note that the original Dry Martini got its name from the fact that it included dry vermouth instead of sweet. This was a common way of describing Cocktails that incorporated vermouth as either a primary or secondary ingredient. The most common Cocktail today that continues this naming convention is the Manhattan. Normally made with sweet vermouth, a Dry Manhattan uses dry vermouth, and a Perfect Manhattan uses equal parts of sweet and dry vermouth. As we have seen reflected in the above recipes, this same naming convention originally applied to the Martini as well.

So we now see that by the very early 1900s the appreciation for Cocktails in general—and the Martini in specific—had arrived at a point where there were slight vari-

---

8. Harry Craddock , *The Savoy Cocktail Book* (London: Richard R. Smith, 1930), p. 62.

9. Ibid. p. 102.

ations in drink recipes. I view this very careful fine-tuning of the Martini as a reflection of the bartenders' craft: to bring out the culinary aspects that can be found in a Cocktail. The ingredients were being carefully blended, balanced and selected in order to result in a drink that was not just a glass of cold gin, but a culinary accomplishment in its own right.

And then came Prohibition.

## THE REALLY DRY YEARS

**P**rohibition—a strange and interesting time in American Cocktail history—was most certainly the catalyst for many changes in the drinking habits of Americans, and in fact the world. Here in America, spirits—and the consumption thereof—went underground. When Americans traveled abroad, their desire for Cocktails in the bars they frequented, such as Harry's American Bar in Paris, or La Floridita in Havana, brought about many interesting changes as bartenders made an effort to cater to these tourists from the New World. Up until this point, Cocktails had been primarily an American pastime. But these thirsty travelers soon convinced foreign establishments to learn this arcane culinary art form.

It was also during this period that Americans really became acquainted with gin. During Prohibition's early days, American rye whiskey appeared to be the most popular spirit. As the "Great Experiment" continued, however, it became far more difficult to properly distill, and, more importantly, age whiskey. Distilling a neutral grain spirit, which doesn't require aging, was fairly easy. To this base spirit, some water was then added to adjust the strength and soften the bite. By adding a little juniper extract, the mixture not only turned it into a passable approximation of gin, the added flavoring also helped to hide some of the remaining harshness or impurities.

During Prohibition, the Cocktail in America lost any semblance of being a culinary accomplishment. Instead it became simply an alcohol-delivery vehicle as well as a commentary on the political atmosphere of the country. It was an escape. It was an excuse. And it was retaliation. But worst of all, it effectively lobotomized an entire generation, deleting from memory what the Cocktail and the Martini were all about.

## OUT THE OTHER SIDE

When Prohibition was repealed in 1933, the public didn't sigh a breath of relief because they could finally get a "good" Cocktail. No. Their relief was because now they could legally get drunk. The drinking public had lost all connection with what a great cocktail was all about. And they had all but forgotten the true Martini. They were in search of direction, of leadership, and hoping that somebody would provide it. Fortunately somebody did. The celebrities of the day—Churchill, Rockefeller, Hemingway, Bogart and many others—were more than willing to provide their interpretation of how to make the best Martini. There are countless descriptions found in popular literature of the day, Churchill was said to prefer "merely glancing at the vermouth while you pour the gin", or "look in the direction of France", while some would simply whisper "vermouth" over the mixing glass. Less known, unfortunately, is that the authors of many of these convoluted methodologies were borderline, if not full-blown alcoholics. It is more likely that they looked at the bottle of gin, then at the bottle of vermouth, and noticed that one was 45 percent alcohol, the other only 17 percent, and they knew exactly how to best increase the amount of personal alcohol consumption.

Even though most of the bartenders guides of the early 1930s continued to list a proper recipe for a Martini, over the next couple of decades the general public insisted on having theirs made the same way as their movie star heroes drank them. Suddenly, the term "dry" was no longer a reference for what type of vermouth to use. Instead, "dry" was a measure of the decreasing amount of vermouth, and the perceived increase in the alcoholic content. Perhaps this was a subtle parody on the use of "dry" to reference being without alcohol, only now the tables were turned and its meaning was reversed.

Coming out of Prohibition, the Martini's evolution appears to have almost been in hibernation. While I expect that during Prohibition all sorts of abominations were served and referred to as a Martini. These did not appear to make it into any of the cocktail books of the day. This quickly changed. Through the 1940s and into the 1950s several major shifts in reality occurred. The use of bitters in Martinis disappeared. Vermouth became less and less important as an ingredient. And the people behind Smirnoff's marketing campaign came up with the concept of substituting vodka for gin in order to increase the sales of their product.

## INTO THE MODERN AGE

The 1960s ushered in an era of free love, free expression and freedom from "the establishment." Cocktails such as the Martini, Manhattan and Old Fashioned were *persona non grata* to this party. Alcohol itself was often passed over in favor of other forms of intoxicants. The focus during these days was more on the achieved effect, instead of the culinary quality of the product itself. When Cocktails and/or wines were considered, they were often chosen for their light and fruity flavor, their inexpensive cost or more often both.

Times were tough for our old friend the Martini. We had still not yet recovered from the cocktail devastation caused by Prohibition. There was little in the way of hope looming on the horizon. Add to this the appearance of vodka to the scene during the 1950s, along with its well-oiled marketing machine, and we suddenly have 1960s screen-sensation James Bond telling us that the proper Martini is not only "shaken, not stirred," but that it should be made with vodka instead of gin. In print however, one of Mr. Bond's first signature drinks has come to be known as the "Vesper" and was described in the very first Bond novel *Casino Royale* thusly: "Three measures of Gordon's, one of vodka, half a measure of Kina Lillet. Shake it very well until it's ice cold, then add a large slice of lemon peel."

By the mid-1980s, people started to re-discover the Martini. The concept of the cocktail had maintained itself, but mostly as "shooters" or drinks with silly, if not provocative names such as Orgasm, Brain Hemorrhage or Freddy Fudpucker. Gary Regan, in his book *The Joy of Mixology*, refers to these concoctions as "Punk Drinks" because "they seemed to be liquid versions of bands like the Sex Pistols—they certainly didn't harmonize well, but they sure as hell made themselves heard."[10] Also around this time, a rallying cry around being "retro" arose, embracing—if not emulating—the fashions, trends, and attitudes of the past. The classic Cocktail began to once again get some attention: if not in actual practice, at least in theatric simulation.

The Martini played an important role here: it served as a conceptual icon for all that embodied a Cocktail, and

---

10. Gary Regan, *The Joy of Mixology: The Consummate Guide to the Bartender's Craft* (New York: Clarkston N. Potter), p. 45.

provided the visual icon of the elegant cocktail glass with its crystal clear purity. But just as the marketing engines of the past told earlier generations it was okay to substitute vodka for gin, the modern marketing establishments latched on to the notion that everybody wanted to drink a Martini and began telling the public that everything they were drinking *was* a Martini.

## MARKETING THE MARTINI

I distinctly remember being at a San Francisco restaurant with a friend around 1995, and ordering a Martini—my drink of choice. My friend looked at me, looked at the waiter, then back at me again. You could see the sparkle in his eye: a Martini, o-o-o-oh. He had never had one. But he wanted to have one. A Martini. That quintessential Cocktail. The drink that James Bond always ordered. Tuxedos. Expensive cars. So I ordered one for him as well. The drink came to the table—crystal clear, light beads of moisture forming on the sides of the glass. A single olive with a crystal-clear pick pierced through its heart. Up to the lips. A sip. *Boing!* His expression immediately changed to shock. *Whoa!* For somebody more accustomed to drinking wine and beer, a modern Martini can represent a very rude awakening into what alcohol actually tastes like. He ended up leaving the drink at only a sip.

But he wanted a Martini. He really did. It represented something special to him. To the uninitiated, even a vodka-based Martini has a flavor profile that is so different from the soda-pops of our youth, that it is an unwelcome shock. In the tradition of giving the customer what they want, 1990s Cocktail lounges across the country started providing variations on the Martini. Whether it was splashes of juice to soften the bite, or unusual ingredients to make them unique, suddenly there were "Martini Menus" popping up all over the place, listing drinks of every possible design. And each one was allegedly a Martini.

Existing Cocktails such as the Lemon Drop, Cosmopolitan and even the Manhattan (which predates the Martini) were suddenly categorized as a Martini. In many cases, any drink that might previously have been called a "Cocktail" was now a type of Martini. To expand this trend, the stemmed cocktail glass itself was rechristened the "Martini glass." Entire books have been written which include hundreds of different so-called Martini recipes. So it is no wonder that there is confusion about what a Martini really is.

## TODAY'S MARTINI

The best way to account for what a Martini is at any point in time, is to try to conceptualize what drink would be served to you if you walked in to a lounge and asked for a Martini: no qualifiers, not brand names, no agendas. As we have seen, this originally would have been a drink consisting of sweet vermouth, (sweet) gin, bitters, maraschino liqueur, and perhaps even garnished with a cherry. Today, if you ask for a Martini, you will most likely receive a drink consisting of cold gin (more likely vodka!) and a cocktail pick laden with green olives. Two drinks that are worlds apart.

Many bartenders these days instinctively leave the vermouth entirely out of the Martinis they make. It's an issue of convenience as well as cost. If a customer sends a Martini back saying it didn't have enough vermouth, it's easy enough to add a quick dash. But if they say it has too much vermouth, you can't take it out. Even so, I have on numerous occasions watched the bartender make a Martini without any vermouth at all, only to have it returned by the customer because it had too much.

Then there are those customers who order a Martini, without any qualifiers, and expect it to be made out of vodka. This has become so common in recent years that somebody who wants a gin Martini needs to be sure to ask for it specifically.

## THE PATH OF ENLIGHTENMENT

I expect we've pretty much hit the bottom of the barrel for where a Martini can go. Once you take everything out of the Martini except the gin (or vodka), it's gotten about as far away from being a Cocktail as it can get. I keep hoping that what we have now is similar to the soda-pop-wine-phase of the 1970s and that customers will soon realize that there is more to a fine Martini then just cold gin. Perhaps eventually the Martini will again become a Cocktail that takes skill and alchemy to construct. Yeah, right. And perhaps bartenders will stop filling my Old Fashioneds with soda.

To bring the Martini, as well as its other Cocktail brethren, back to the point where they represent something more then just an alcohol-delivery vehicle, it would be necessary to return it to its position as a culinary art form. The Cocktail is, in fact, a cuisine—and a distinctly American cuisine at that. When properly executed, it should exhibit the same complexities of ingredients, balance of flavors, and attention to construction plus presentation as would be expected from any master French chef.

As we saw in the earlier recipes, the Martini was once a drink of carefully-combined ingredients that needed to be meticulously mastered in order to be fully appreciated.

While many of the products we have available to us today differ greatly from the products used in the original Martinis, we can still learn from their construction and re-discover this forgotten classic.

## A JOURNEY OF SELF-DISCOVERY

I could simply spout off what I felt was the correct recipe for a Martini. But all you would then be doing is following my lead. My preference would be that you discover for yourself what you feel provides the best culinary experience—and why.

To start with, you need to gather the proper ingredients. I don't care if you are a Vodka Martini drinker or not. For this Cocktail you need to use gin and a good gin at that: Plymouth, Hendricks, Boodles, Tanqueray, Bombay or some other gin, if you think you have a specific preference. If your preferred gin costs less then $15, I recommend that you pick one of the premium brands I listed above. Next, you will need a bottle of dry vermouth. Noilly Prat is my favorite. There are, of course, others such as Cinzano or Martini & Rossi. If you've got a bottle already but it has been getting dusty in your cupboard, you should probably pick up a fresh one. Vermouth after all is a wine, and while it is slightly fortified (which aids in longevity), that doesn't mean it is immortal.

Lastly, if there is any way you can get a hold of some orange bitters, I highly recommend it. Angostura or Peychaud bitters are unfortunately not a substitute. Fee Brothers (http://www.FeeBrothers.com) is one source for this.

For equipment, you will need a mixing glass or standard pint beer glass, a long teaspoon or stirring stick (a chopstick works well in a pinch), a cocktail strainer, several stemmed cocktail glasses and plenty of fresh ice. Ice that has been sitting around in your freezer is spending most of its time just soaking up all of the random odor in there, clearly not a component to a quality Cocktail.

You are now going to mix up several different variations of the Martini, each one using a different ratio of ingredients. You are going to mix them all up, one after the other, placing each drink in the freezer while you prepare the next and the next. When you are finished mixing, you are going to taste them all in succession.

Mix each drink by filling the mixing glass half-full of ice, then pouring in the liquid ingredients. Stir the drink well, making sure to get as much movement of the ice within the liquid as possible. Two important things are happening at this stage. Not only is the ice chilling the liquid down, the ice is also melting and adding water to the drink. This water is an extremely important ingredient to making the drink properly, which is why you should not store your spirits in the refrigerator or freezer.

Here are the series of drinks you are going to prepare:

Drink #1:  Make this one with straight gin. Don't add any dry vermouth at all.

Drink #2:  Use an 8:1 ratio for this one. That means 8 parts gin to one part dry vermouth. Or to put this in measurement terms, use two ounces gin and one-quarter ounce dry vermouth.

Drink #3:  Use a 4:1 ratio this time. Or 2 ounces gin and one-half ounce dry vermouth.

Drink #4:  Make this one with straight dry vermouth.

Notice that I don't say anything about garnish here. Any garnish—olive or lemon twist—will slightly change the flavor. We are mostly concerned, right now, with understanding the balance issues with the main ingredients. You don't want to be sidetracked by the brine or other flavors that might be added by the garnish.

Now comes the fun part. Carefully taste each drink. Take a sip from each one in turn. Try to forget what you think a Martini should taste like. Instead, pay attention to the balance of the ingredients. Don't be judgmental at the onset. Just try to see if you can notice a difference of any sort amongst them. Keep going back through the flight of Cocktails. Gradually try to pay attention to the balance in the flavors. You should, of course, notice that the first one tastes like total gin, with no dry vermouth flavor at all. In the third drink, you should be able to detect enough dry vermouth to get an idea of what its flavor does for the Cocktail overall. And the last drink will, of course, taste like straight vermouth. Pay specific attention to the middle drinks. Do they taste like they have too much gin or too much vermouth?

The important question, of course, is which one did you like best? Which one tasted like it was the most balanced: not too much gin, not too much vermouth. If you look at the ratios involved, you'll see that there is quite difference between them. Also notice that Drink #3 definitely isn't as far as you can take it. The goal here is for you to determine what your favorite gin-to-vermouth ratio is. If you liked Drink #3 the best, maybe you'd like even more vermouth? In that case, you should try another round (perhaps tomorrow night), using even more vermouth. Keep adding more and more, until you feel you've gone too far.

Or if you liked Drink #2 the best, perhaps a little experimentation with ratios on either side of this recipe is what you need to focus your attention on. Remember: You are looking for a balance of flavors here. You are trying to detect that point where the flavors of the gin and the vermouth almost reach a point where you can't tell where one flavor stops, and the other one begins.

Now, once you have arrived at what you feel is just the right ratio of gin to vermouth, make this cocktail again, and this time include a dash of orange bitters. Despite its name, you won't find that this adds a bitter—or even an orange—flavor to the drink. Instead it will bring about just a hint of added complexity, which just further enhances the Martini's culinary appeal and sophistication, thus, returning this drink back to its origins as a culinary accomplishment and as a Cocktail in the classic style.

## MARTINI FUTURES

We've seen how the Martini started out as a drink that took a while to discover its own unique identity, and how it eventually blossomed into a respected and popular libation by the early 1900s. This emergence was cut short by Prohibition, which proved to be a catastrophic blow to the recognition and understanding of the Cocktail as an American cuisine. Today, the Martini suffers the injustice of being wildly popular, but only because of a case of mistaken identity. Can the Martini be saved? Can it be once again perceived and understood as a Cocktail of culinary precision?

For guidance, I look at the way wine and beer have each been able to make significant gains in both quality and appreciation over the last couple of decades. These two Prohibition refugees were also once pale shadows of their former selves. But recently they have re-emerged and have even surpassed the craftsmanship and notoriety that had been their legacies. I would like to think that we are just now seeing a similar resurgence in the appreciation and understanding of the Cocktail. And that soon we will once again be able to regularly find drinks coming from the bar, which reflect the same culinary standards being served forth from the kitchens of our favorite restaurants.

## FURTHER READING

In addition to simply referring to various old bartenders' guides to learn more about how the Martini and other cocktails have evolved/devolved over time, I recommend the following books which contain useful insights and information. They were valuable in providing me with guidance and inspiration for portions of this article:

Edmunds, Lowell, *Martini, Straight Up: The Classic American Cocktail.* (Baltimore: Johns Hopkins University Press, 1998).

Grimes, William, *Straight Up or On the Rocks: The Story of the American Cocktail.* (New York: North Point Press, 2001).

Regan, Gary, *The Joy of Mixology: The Consummate Guide to the Bartender's Craft.* (New York: Clarkson N. Potter, 2003).

Regan, Gary and Mardee, *The Martini Companion: A Connoisseur's Guide.* (Philadelphia: Running Press Books, 1997).

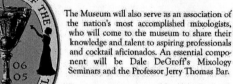

# HISTORY AND CHARACTER OF THE GIMLET

BY PAUL CLARKE

*The Gimlet sailed the Seven Seas along with the officers and ship's surgeons who drank them regularly in hopes of staving off scurvy. Originally made with gin and preserved lime juice cordial, the Gimlet has evolved in its current resurgence and reinvention. Paul Clarke examines both the alleged origins of the Gimlet; the history of its most distinctive ingredient, Rose's Lime Juice Cordial; and the modifications and personal touches that have entered into this classic Cocktail vernacular up to present day.*

**I**F THE MARTINI IS THE DAVID NIVEN of the Cocktail universe, the Gimlet is Robert Mitchum. With its ethereal, pale-green appearance and slightly sweet, slightly funky flavor, the Gimlet is hard enough and sharp enough to get the job done. But while capable of occasional brilliance, at its core it's an Everyman with little use for frippery. That this humble concoction of spirits and sweetened lime juice has managed to establish itself on the permanent roster of classic cocktails is something of a surprise. After all, the Gimlet has neither the nuance nor sophistication of a Martini or Manhattan. Nor does it carry a vaguely festive or carefree aura, as with a Daiquiri or Planter's Punch. Instead, the Gimlet is a determined hard-worker: A Cocktail that's been described as "the king of the well drinks." Likely born in a sailor's cup and once common throughout the British Empire's furthest reaches, the Gimlet is resilient enough to survive at the hands of even the most novice of bartenders, and simple enough to make them think they can mix one without doing serious harm. In bars that have witnessed the silent deaths of countless once-trendy Cocktails, the Gimlet is a survivor.

If the Gimlet is not actually a British creation, it certainly deserves honorary citizenship. There is widespread—if not universal—agreement that the Gimlet is a product of the Royal Navy. The first Gimlet-like beverage was probably concocted in the years following passage of the Merchant Shipping Act of 1867, which mandated that British merchant ships carry daily rations of lime juice for the crew to combat scurvy.[2] (Naval ships had been under similar

---

1. See http://webmonkey.wired.com/cocktail/97/15/index4a.html)
2. *Cambridge World History of Food*, ed. Kenneth F. Kiple, Kriemhild Conee Ornelas (Cambridge: Cambridge University Press, 2000.

requirements for several decades). That same year, a Scottish merchant named Lauchlin Rose patented a process of preserving lime juice without the use of alcohol.[3] This development, combined with the requirements of the new law, meant that Rose's Lime Juice Cordial was soon widespread throughout the British Empire.

Given the mandated lime juice ration, along with the daily ration of spirits (rum was still a staple, though gin was also common and favored by many officers), it was probably inevitable that the two liquids would eventually find their way into the same cup. But credit for first mixing the juice with gin is typically given to a surgeon, Sir Thomas D. Gimlette, who joined the navy in 1879 and retired as Surgeon General in 1913.[4] Popular lore has it that Gimlette, an officer, induced his messmates to take their antiscorbutic by mixing it with gin, and the new concoction was named in his honor. A related theory posits that Gimlette was concerned with his men's heavy drinking, so he diluted their gin with lime juice. While this likely would have done little to reduce their overall consumption, it did make for a more flavorful beverage, and the new drink was duly anointed with his name.

A rival theory suggests that the drink was named for the corkscrew-like tool that was reportedly sent with lime juice containers to British colonies during the late eighteenth century. However, pre-1867 shipments of lime juice were typically preserved by adding demerara rum,[5] so mixing this juice with gin would have been both potent and probably unpalatable.

---

4. See the Royal Navy website, http://www.royal-navy.mod.uk/rn/ content. php3?page=4748.

5. David I. Harvie, *Limeys: The True Story of One Man's War Against Ignorance, the Establishment and the Deadly Scurvy* (Gloucestershire: Sutton Publishing Limited, 2002.

While either of these theories are possible and one of them is likely true for the origin of the name "Gimlet," two other points are worth considering. The first comes from the Royal Navy's Maritime Museum, which notes that although Gimlette is commonly credited with creating the drink, neither his 1943 obituary in *The Times* nor his entry in *Who Was Who 1941-1950*[6] mention any connection with the drink, which by the time of his death had become quite popular.

The second point concerns the early appearances in bar manuals of gimlet-like drinks under similar, though different names. The first known appearance of a Gimlet relative appeared in *The Ideal Bartender*,[7] a 1917 manual by Tom Bullock, a bartender from St. Louis. In his guide, he lists a recipe for a "Gillette Cocktail, Chicago Style," composed of fresh lime juice, sugar, and Old Tom gin, stirred with ice and served straight up in a cocktail glass. While the use of fresh lime and sugar (as opposed to a prepared, sweetened lime juice) isn't the recipe typically thought of as a "true" Gimlet, by mixing the drink without seltzer—thus distinguishing it from a Sweet Gin Rickey—Bullock was pouring a cocktail that was distinctly related to the drink now known as a Gimlet. While the origins of the name "Gillette Cocktail, Chicago Style" will likely remain a mystery, the appellation seems too similar to Gimlet to be purely a coincidence.

Bullock's alternative spelling of the name could be just a fluke, but another related yet different spelling appeared a few years later—this time in the company of a recipe for another drink dubbed a "Gimlet." Harry Crad-

---

6. National Maritime Museum website, http://www.nmm.ac.uk.

7. Tom Bullock, *173 Pre-Prohibition Cocktails: Potations So Good They Scandalized a President* (reproduction of *The Ideal Bartender*, 1917) (Jenks, OK: Howling at the Moon Press, 2001).

dock's *The Savoy Cocktail Book*[8] (which reportedly cribbed heavily from Harry MacElhone's *Harry's ABCs of Mixing Cocktails*[9]), presented two related recipes. The first is for the "Gimblet Cocktail," composed of one part fresh lime juice to three parts dry gin, topped with seltzer (in other words, a Gin Rickey sans ice); and the second is for the "Gimlet Cocktail," made of equal parts Plymouth Gin and Rose's Lime Juice Cordial, stirred and served in the same glass, with or without ice. Near identical recipes were also published in Patrick Gavin Duffy's *The Official Mixer's Manual*.[10]

In a recent online discussion in the eGullet forum dedicated to Cocktails and spirits, Cocktail authority David Wondrich theorized that the US recipe—that is, Bullock's—was an attempt to reproduce British versions of the drink without the use of Rose's Lime Juice Cordial.[11] This product, while then available in Bombay, Singapore and Shanghai, was probably less common in St. Louis, where Bullock tended bar. In the absence of corroborating evidence, it's impossible to determine if Wondrich is correct— though, his theory is compelling, and it's easy to believe that Bullock and other American bartenders were eager to approximate a libation that was gaining popularity in other parts of the globe.

8. Harry Craddock , *The Savoy Cocktail Book* (London: Richard R. Smith, 1930).

9. Harry MacElhone, *Harry's ABCs of Mixing Cocktails* (London: Dean & Son, 1919).

10. Patrick Gavin Duffy, *The Official Mixer's Manual* (New York: R. Long and RR. Smith, 1934). This book was reprinted with the lengthier title, *The Official Mixer's Manual: The Standard Guide for Professional and Amateur bartenders Throughout the World* (Garden City NY: Garden City Books, 1948).

11. EGullet Forum on Fine Spirits and Cocktails (http://forums.egullet.com)

O f course, without the preponderance of pre-served lime juice onboard British ships, it's possible the Gimlet would never have gained the prominence it enjoyed in the mid-twentieth century. But the patenting of Rose's Lime Juice Cordial the same year that lime juice was mandated aboard all British merchant ships was not entirely coincidence. Lauchlin Rose's ancestors had a deep and historic connection with the Royal Navy and the merchant shipping fleet. In the early nineteenth century, the Rose family were one of many involved in small-scale shipbuilding in Leith, the oldest (and, for centuries, only) port in Scotland. This changed in 1859, when Rose & Company relinquished its shipbuilding and turned its attention to ship victualling and foreign trade.

At the time, British naval vessels were required to carry rations of lemon juice to prevent scurvy among the crew. Lemons were typically purchased from suppliers in the Mediterranean. This gradually shifted to limes by 1840, becaues English lime-growers in the West Indies lobbied for the substitution of lime juice for lemon juice on British ships. By 1860, military regulations made the shift official (with disastrous consequences: unknown at the time, lemons contain nearly four times the anti-scorbutic properties of limes, and outbreaks of scurvy continued into the twentieth century).

Of course, fresh limes and lime juice are perishable, and methods were needed to preserve the juice for long periods at sea. In the mid-nineteenth century, the primary method of preservation was to fortify the juice with 15 percent demerara rum. The mixture was then supplied in sealed four-gallon jars.

Around 1865, Lauchlin Rose began focusing on efforts to preserve lime juice without the use of alcohol. Rose had his eye on the shipping trade, and hoped to provide a juice-rich product undiluted by alcohol. But he also hoped to design a product that would fill a niche in the greater marketplace: at the time, non-alcoholic fruit drinks—or a soft-drink industry, for that matter—didn't exist. These efforts were fulfilled in 1867, when Rose registered a patent for preserving lime (and other) juices without using alcohol. His principal patent proposed to use "sulphurous acid or sulphurous gas," which would either be mixed with the juice and allowed to stand, or circulated over and through the juice in air-tight vessels. This exposure of the juice to a sulphur dioxide solution prevented fermentation and other defects in the juice.

Rose struck gold. By 1879, he had registered another nine patents for improved bottles and stoppers, and his Rose's Lime Juice Cordial was embraced both by the Admiralty and by the general public. His popular product was packaged in distinctive leaf-and-lime-embossed bottles, and became the one of the earliest mass-produced soft drinks on the market.

Today, Rose's still dominates the bottled lime juice market. The company, which was purchased by Schweppes in 1957 (now CadburySchweppes plc), claims to account for more than 99 percent of US retail lime-juice sales. And while some modern mixologists may loathe the taste of Rose's (as reflected in an online discussion on the eGullet Cocktails forum), others enjoy the product's unique appearance and flavor, and Paul Harrington, co-author of *Cocktail: The Drinks Bible for the 21st Century*, has proclaimed it "one of the world's great man-made inventions, ranking just under polyester."

Two related products are available in the United States today: Rose's Lime Juice, which is reconstituted lime juice (obtained from limes grown primarily in South America) mixed with high-fructose corn syrup and coloring; and Rose's Lime Cordial, which contains additional sweetener and what a product developer for Schweppes terms "additional essences." Neither product contains alcohol. In a taste comparison, the cordial is sweeter and has less lime intensity. In addition, the company produces an unsweetened version of the lime juice which is available in Canada. Most product available in North America is made in Upstate New York; the company also maintains facilities in Denmark and Finland. Versions of Rose's obtained elsewhere in the world are mostly similar to that found in the US, with the key distinction being the increased use of sucrose—granulated sugar—to sweeten the European-made juice, versus the high-fructose corn syrup used in the United States.

But questions remain about the taste of Rose's in a Gimlet, and if today's product tastes the same as that on the market in the early twentieth century. The question first arises from drink recipes such as those published by Craddock and Duffy in the 1930s, which call for much greater proportions of Rose's Lime Juice Cordial than do today's recipes—consider Craddock's 1930 recipe calling for a 1:1 ratio of gin to Rose's, versus the greater than 3:1 ratio found in Gary Regan's *The Joy of Mixology*[12] (Regan's recipe calls for the juice, as opposed to the cordial, which results in an even drier cocktail than that suggested by Craddock). Another intriguing point is brought up by Charles H. Baker who, in *The Gentleman's Companion*,[13] wrote that Rose's Lime Syrup "is a pungent oil-of-lime syrup coming in tall, slender, decorative bottles so often seen behind good soda fountains. It is indicated in the Gimlet Cocktail, and bears a lot of experimentation [...] Lime Cor-

---

12. Gary Regan, *The Joy of Mixology: The Consummate Guide to the Bartender's Craft* (New York: Clarkston N. Potter).

13. Charles H. Baker, *The Gentleman's Companion, Vol. II: Being an Exotic Drinking Book or Around the World with Jigger, Beaker, and Flask* (New York: Crown Publishers, 1946)

dial can be made by mixing this about half and half with gomme syrup." In his Gimlet recipe, Baker calls for the use of 1 jigger of dry or Old Tom gin, combined with one-half teaspoon (to taste) of lime syrup or cordial—which, he writes, "is a British invention based on a similar essence to Rose's Lime Juice [...] but is not quite so pungent."—and another teaspoon of sugar or gomme syrup. Using the Rose's Lime Juice (or cordial) commonly found in the US market today, with the sweetened Old Tom gin and added sugar Baker indicates, would likely result in a very sweet drink.

Why is there such discrepancy between the amount of Rose's Lime Juice (or cordial) called for in early Gimlet recipes as compared to those published today? And even in recipes such as Baker's, that have a smaller proportion of lime juice, why was additional sweetener desired? At first, it seems as though the answer may lie with Rose's—perhaps reformulations over the years may have increased the product's sweetness, thus making smaller amounts of it more desirable in Cocktails. But Tony Livaich, a Connecticut-based product developer for Schweppes, believes that the formula and flavor of Rose's products have changed very little over the past century (with the exception of the switch to high-fructose corn syrup as a sweetener for the US-made product, which Livaich maintains makes a negligible difference in flavor).[14] While the difference could be due to a preference at the time for sweeter Cocktails (or a belief that the Gimlet should be a sweet Cocktail), it's also likely that a couple of basic mixological differences are at play.

First, the Gimlet recipes cited by Craddock and Duffy both called for the use of Plymouth Gin, in equal concentration to the amount of Rose's. As David Wondrich

---

14. Personal telephone communications with Tony Livaich, September 30, 2004.

pointed out in the previously mentioned eGullet online discussion, the Plymouth Gin found aboard naval ships of the era was quite strong—between 109° and 116° proof, by the US system—so, without the aid of ice for dilution, more lime juice would have been desired to make the mixture palatable. Second, for recipes such as Baker's, it's possible that the reference was to an unsweetened version of Rose's (such as that sold in Canada today)—the "pungent oil-of-lime syrup" he mentions. The same could possibly be true for Boothby,[15] who does not specify a brand but simply calls for equal parts gin and "lime syrup."

Without further details from these early cocktail guides, it's impossible to determine exactly what product was being used to concoct their Gimlets. But regardless of the sweetness level of Gimlets in the 1930s, by the 1940s, gin was gaining the upper hand in the ratio of Gimlet recipes. A step in this direction can be seen in Vic Bergeron's *Trader Vic's Book of Food and Drink*,[16] with its 1.5:1 ratio of gin to Rose's Lime Juice (though Bergeron does add a teaspoon of sugar—again, without indicating if it's an unsweetened version of Rose's he is using). The ratio jumps further in *Esquire's Handbook for Hosts*,[17] which doubles Bergeron's ratio and eliminates the extra sugar.

Around this time, the Gimlet also took an unusual, though apparently limited detour away from lime juice altogether: in the 1958 edition of *The Fine Art of Mixing Drinks*,[18] David Embury writes that the Orange Blossom—gin, orange juice and simple syrup—is sometimes incor-

---

15. William Boothby, *"Cocktail Bill" Boothby's World Drinks and How to Mix Them* (San Francisco: The Recorder Printing and Publishing, 1934).

16. Vic Bergeron, *Trader Vic's Book of Food and Drink* (Garden City, NY: Doubleday, 1946).

17. *Esquire's Handbook for Hosts* (New York: Grosset & Dunlop, 1949).

18. David Embury, *The Fine Art of Mixing Drinks* (Garden City, NY: Garden City Books, 1958).

rectly called a Gimlet. "Actually," Embury writes, "the Gimlet is a Gin Rickey and is made with sugar, lime juice, gin and carbonated water." As credence to Embury's correction, this orange-based variation appears around that time in *The Stork Club Bar Book*,[19] in which a Gimlet is composed of equal parts gin and orange juice, shaken with ice and served straight up.

The serving method for the gimlet has also varied over time. Bullock, Boothby and Bergeron all suggest serving a Gimlet (and its relations) straight up in a cocktail glass. Other variations suggest serving it with a dash of soda (*Esquire*) or plain water (Baker), and served in Delmonico or old-fashioned glasses (Duffy and Craddock) or even a saucer champagne glass (Baker), with or without ice.

Today, most influential bar manuals suggest serving Gimlets on the dry side—such as Gary Regan's greater than 3:1 ratio, or Dale DeGroff's 5:1 ratio from *The Craft of the Cocktail*.[20] But, while the ratio of spirits to lime juice has remained mostly stable for the past 50 years, a sea change has also occurred in the Gimlet's composition. At the time of the Gimlet's peak popularity in the mid-twentieth century, asking a bartender for a "Gin Gimlet" was as redundant as asking for a "Gin Martini." But during the vodka revolution in late-twentieth-century mixology, Gimlets were redefined, and many, if not most, are now mixed with vodka.[21] Add to this a constant drive to alter and expand on existing recipes, and the Gimlet has changed in ways unimaginable to early bartenders. Ingredients such as triple sec and cranberry juice have been added to Vodka Gimlets, spawning Cocktail trends such as those of the

19. Lucius Beebe, *The Stork Club Bar Book* (New York: Rinehart & Company, 1946).

20. Dale DeGroff, *The Craft of the Cocktail* (New York: Clarkson N. Potter, 2002).

21. Personal email communications with Tony Abou-Ganim, September 29, 2004.

Kamikaze and Cosmopolitan. With the shift from gin to vodka, anything seemed possible, and Gimlets made with white rum or silver tequila have appeared on Cocktail menus with greater frequency.

Riding this wave of change, Rose's corporate parents launched the website www.rosesgimlet.com, which offers recipes for ten different types of Gimlet, ranging from the classic White Gimlet to concoctions containing vanilla vodka and melon liqueur (the Emerald Gimlet), strawberry vodka and grenadine (the Ruby Gimlet) and even coconut rum and crème de cacao (the Diamond Gimlet, served in a glass rimmed with white-chocolate ganache)—and all including Rose's Lime Juice.[22]

While such drinks are certain to appeal to the younger demographics that corporate marketers have in mind, there are also signs that the Gimlet is being rediscovered, and is sometimes appearing in different manifestations. Some restaurants, such as Daniel in New York, apply the mantra of freshness to their bars and serve Gimlets using only fresh lime juice and simple syrup.[23] Bemelman's Bar at New York's Carlyle Hotel uses Rose's in its Gimlets, but Beverage Director Audrey Saunders also suggests trying the drink with a lime-infused syrup, mixed with fresh lime juice in the shaker. For the syrup, Saunders adds the zest from one lime to one cup of simple syrup, and strains the infusion after 24 hours (or to taste). When combined with fresh lime juice and mixed with gin, the drink has a fresh lime intensity notably absent from Gimlets made with Rose's, but with a depth and complexity not found in a similar drink made with syrup without the lime infusion.

---

22. Robert Plotkin, "Sizzling Hot Gimlets," *Restaurant Hospitality*, May 2000.
23. Leslie Brenner, *The Fourth Star: Dispatches from Inside Daniel Boulud's Celebrated New York Restaurant* (New York: Clarkson N. Potter, 2002).

Contemporary Cocktail masters such as Tony Abou-Ganim[24] admit that Gimlets made with Rose's Lime Juice lack the same flavor as those made with fresh lime juice. But, says Abou-Ganim, "I try to retain as much of a drinks heritage and honor the original recipes." Since authenticity matters, Abou-Ganim uses the bottled juice in his Gimlets (though he does add a squeeze of fresh lime). "I will say that a Cocktail made with fresh-squeezed lime juice and simple syrup is a wonderful Cocktail," he says, "but, give the Rose's folks their due and honor the recipe as I feel it was first mixed."

If the Gimlet was first mixed at a time when Britain was at its pinnacle, it also appeared late in the day, as the sun prepared to set on the Empire. The drink's ubiquity in eastern colonial outposts give it a hint of exoticism, but its role as a bystander in a tragically changing world also lend it a jaded, Graham Greene-type personality. These characteristics have made the Gimlet a notable bit player in mid- and late-twentieth century literature. Writers as varied as William Trevor, Chester Himes and Bret Easton Ellis have used the Gimlet as a device, a drink sad and alien, marking turbulence and trouble.

In Ernest Hemingway's short story "The Short Happy Life of Francis Macomber,"[25] Gimlets are used by his troubled trio of lion hunters to wash away the taste of cowardice and disgust following a shameful day in the bush.

---

24. Personal email communications with Tony Abou-Ganim, September 29, 2004.
25. "The Short Happy Life of Francis Macomber" in Ernest Hemingway, *The Short Stories* (New York: Scribner, 1995).

For David Mamet, Gimlets are the drink of the prey: in the play, *Glengarry Glen Ross*,[26] an unsuspecting and weak-willed client drinks Gimlets while a predatory real-estate salesman sets him up for the hard-sell. Wallace Stegner's protagonist in the short story "Something Spurious from the Mindanao Deep"[27] broods over a string of Gimlets in Manila while coming to terms with an embittered sense of humanity: "All men were human but their humanity took very different forms; and to insist on overlooking the differences was to come finally to [...] a reliance on the Gimlet to get you from breakfast to lunch, from lunch to dinner, and from dinner to bed."

But as hard-bitten as these literary Cocktails may be, a play with an even more jaded worldview ridicules Gimlets (in the same breath as pousse-cafés) as mere training wheels on a cocktail glass. In Edward Albee's play *Who's Afraid of Virginia Woolf?*, a liquor-sodden night begins to spiral out of control shortly after George mocks his wife Martha's early drink preferences to a pair of new acquaintances, while pouring her one in a long series of strong drinks of straight liquor:

> Back when I was courting Martha, she'd order the damnedest things! [...] We'd go into a bar...you know, a bar...a whiskey, beer, and bourbon bar...and what she'd do would be, she'd screw up her face, think real hard, and come up with...Brandy Alexanders, Crème de Cacao Frappes, Gimlets, flaming punch bowls...seven-layer liqueur things. [...] But the years have brought to Martha a sense of essentials...the knowledge that cream is for coffee, lime juice for pies...and alcohol pure and

26. David Mamet, *Glengarry Glen Ross* (New York: Samuel French, Inc. 1982).
27. "Something Spurious from the Mindanao Deep" in Wallace Stegner, *Collected Stories of Wallace Stegner* (New York: Penguin, 1990).

simple—here you are, angel—for the pure and simple.[28]

But perhaps no other work uses the Gimlet as extensively and to as much effect as does Raymond Chandler's noir novel *The Long Goodbye.*[29] Gimlets serve as a bonding mechanism between the doomed Terry Lennox and Chandler's legendary detective Philip Marlowe. Lennox is particular about his drinks: "'They don't know how to make them here,' he said. 'What they call a Gimlet is just some lime or lemon juice and gin with a dash of sugar and bitters. A real Gimlet is half gin and half Rose's Lime Juice and nothing else. It beats Martinis hollow.'"

As with Stegner's protagonist, Lennox and Marlowe prefer to drink their Gimlets in the late afternoon, before the bars are filled with people. After Lennox disappears in Mexico and Marlowe believes he's dead, he keeps returning to the bar they used to frequent, to sip Gimlets and brood. As Chandler—who had a taste for Gimlets himself[30]—keeps returning to the drink throughout the novel, he gives Marlowe the opportunity to embark on extended ruminations on the complexity of the world around him, which becomes even more inscrutable as the plot proceeds to its grim conclusion.

In *The Long Goodbye*, the Gimlet lives up to its full jaded-tough potential: simple, strong and pungent, a drink that's made for brooding, but has no use for sentiment. Like Marlowe, the Gimlet survives the challenges that come its way. And while it's a favorite for lonesome protagonists such as Marlowe and Stegner's Robert Burns, the Gimlet also lends itself to company. Functioning as what author

---

28. Edward Albee, *Who's Afraid of Virginia Woolf?* (New York: Signet, 1983).

29. Raymond Chandler, *The Long Goodbye* (original copyright 1953) (New York: Vintage Crime/Black Lizard, 1992).

30. Tom Hiney, *Raymond Chandler* (New York: Grove Press, 1999).

Joseph Lanza calls "a beacon for disaster,"[31] the Gimlet does what any foil in a noir novel should do: set Marlowe on the path for future trouble. "The bartender set the drink in front of me. With the lime juice it has a sort of pale greenish yellowish misty look. I tasted it. It was both sweet and sharp at the same time. The woman in black watched me. Then she lifted her own glass towards me. We both drank. Then I knew hers was the same drink."

---

31. Joseph Lanza, *The Cocktail: The Influence of Spirits on the American Psyche* (New York: Picador USA, 1995).

# The GENEALOGY
# and MYTHOLOGY
## of the
# SINGAPORE SLING

BY TED "DR. COCKTAIL" HAIGH

*Pretty and pink, the Singapore Sling has quenched thirsty British Colonial palates at Singapore's famed Raffles Hotel since 1915, when it was known as the Straits Sling. Ted Haigh warns readers not to dismiss this libation as another "Tiki" creation made by westerners to satisfy their desire to taste Paradise. He traces this tropical quencher from its island roots back to its true origins as the seventeenth-century Sling and then offers readers a point of revelation. The sweet, fruity Singapore Slings most of us have experienced has little in common with its spicy and soda-less ancestors.*

**W**HEN IT COMES TO DRINKS and drinking, it is well established (in a little continuing joke on history) that myth is reality, or at least becomes so after several potent libations. When scant years after its origin no one can agree on who coined the Cosmopolitan (though there are many claimants), there can be little doubt that mixology inhabits a particularly fanciful corner of our universe.

The bejeweled trophy for myth-as-reality in drinks must go to the genre of drinks we know as Tiki. The tropical drink was created out of whole cloth by Americans to feed our balmy fantasies of paradise. Even the drinks we consider most genuinely tropical were created not by native islanders, but by Europeans first then Americans. The (Rum) Swizzle would be an example of the former and, of course, Mai Tai and Zombie the latter.

That said, if ever there was a drink close to real—created in the tropics, albeit to serve the tastes of its colonial guests—it was the Singapore Sling. But what was it? The red, fruity fantasia presented as a Singapore Sling for the better part of the drink's history is really an extension, not of the realities of the place, but of the eternal myth. It is not a Sling. And after all these years, it must be revealed that it has also been hiding out under a pseudonym. The original drink made famous by the city-state of Singapore was the Straits Sling. It was this drink that—in or around 1915—a bartender named Ngiam Tong Boon at Raffles Hotel's Long Bar introduced to the world. Sin-

---

1. From http://www.drinkboy.com/Cocktails/recipes/SingaporeSling.html which also contains a reproduction of the Singapore Sling recipe card from Raffles Hotel's Long Bar.

gapore was known as—and so remains today—the Straits Settlements. Locals like the Hainan Chinese bartender Ngiam Tong Boon would've known it that way.

Sometime between 1922 and 1930, the drink took on the more euphonious-sounding name "Singapore Sling" and "Straits Sling" dropped from common usage sometime thereafter—around 1936. The transition was anything but orderly. Apart from the name change, at some point the original recipe was lost and how the drink is made has been a matter of conjecture ever since. Even the Long Bar uses a recipe that dates approximately 21 years after the drink's presumed creation—and that recipe was penned by a patron! This is what they say about it in current literature:

> Originally the Singapore Sling was meant as a woman's drink, hence the attractive pink colour. Today, it is very definitely a drink enjoyed by all, without which any visit to Raffles Hotel is incomplete.
>
> 
>
> 30 ml Gin
> 15 ml Cherry Brandy
> 120 ml Pineapple Juice
> 15 ml Lime Juice
> 7.5 ml Cointreau
> 7.5 ml Dom Benedictine
> 10 ml Grenadine
> A Dash of Angostura Bitters
> Garnish with a slice of Pineapple and Cherry[1]
>
> 

Once lost, however, a great number of recipes have circulated and have varied widely on several points:
- the inclusion or exclusion of water, sparkling or still.

---

2. Harry Craddock , *The Savoy Cocktail Book* (London: Richard R. Smith, 1930).
3. Ibid.

- the inclusion or exclusion of Benedictine
- the inclusion or exclusion of pineapple juice and other fruit juices
- the type of so-called cherry brandy.

Harry Craddock, author of *The Savoy Cocktail Book*, was the first to publish a recipe (without comment) under the name "Singapore Sling." To add to the confusion, he also listed the drink under the name "The Straits Sling," served in punch-fashion for six people. The main difference in his recipes, besides the volume, was in the Benedictine he listed in the Straits Sling formula—but not that of the Singapore Sling:

### SINGAPORE SLING
The Juice of one quarter lemon
one quarter Dry Gin
one half Cherry Brandy
Shake well and strain into medium size glass, and fill with soda water. Add one lump of ice.[2]

### STRAITS SLING (6 PEOPLE)
Place in a shaker 4 glasses of gin, I glass of Benedictine, I glass of Cherry Brandy, the juice of 2 Lemons, a teaspoonful of Angostura Bitters and one of Orange Bitters. Shake sufficiently and serve in large glasses, filling up with Soda Water.[3]

By the time writer, bon vivant and world traveler, Charles Baker had his say about it in 1939, the drinks had evidently again become one. In his book, *The Gentleman's Companion, Vol. II—or Around the World with Jigger, Beaker*

---

4. Charles H. Baker, *The Gentleman's Companion, Vol. II: Being an Exotic Drinking Book or Around the World with Jigger, Beaker, and Flask* (New York: Crown Publishers, 1946).

5. Dale De Groff, *The Craft of the Cocktail* (New York: Clarkson N. Potter, 2002).

*& Flask*, Baker spoke of the recipe he encountered in 1926, and asserted it to be the original:

> The original formula is one third each of dry gin, cherry brandy and Benedictine; shake it for a moment, or stir it in a bar glass, With 2 fairly large lumps of ice to chill. Turn into a small 10 oz highball glass with one lump of ice left in and fill up to individual taste with chilled club soda. Garnish with the spiral peel of 1 green lime. In other ports in the Orient drinkers often use C & C ginger ale instead of soda, or even stone bottle ginger beer.[4]

This is obviously different than the Raffles recipe as it's currently prepared. Famed bartender Dale Degroff would further roil the waters by stating he had received a fax from Raffles' head bartender several years ago as the original recipe:

> 3 ounces pineapple juice
> 1.5 ounces gin
> 0.25 ounce lime juice
> 0.5 ounce Cherry Heering
> 0.25 ounce. Benedictine
> 0.25 ounce Cointreau
> 1 dash Angostura bitters
> Shake with ice, strain. Top with a little soda water.
> Garnish with a flag.[5]

It must be reasserted here, however, that Raffles no longer has the original recipe: a fact that was recorded by the hotel's biographer and by the Communications Department of Raffles Hotel itself. In fact, no one today has documentation to positively confirm the original secret recipe. Nonetheless, what—if anything—precludes any of

---

6. Edward R. Emerson, *Beverages Past & Present* (New York: G. P. Putnam's Sons, 1908)

7. *The Slang Dictionary: Etymological, Historical, and Anecdotal* (London: John Camden Hotten/Chatto & Windus, 1874).

8. William Terrington, *Cooling Cups and Dainty Drinks* (London and New York: G. Routledge and Sons, 1869).

these recipes from possibly being the inaugural Sling from Singapore?

To answer this, it is first helpful to examine what, specifically Slings were and were not:

Several Slings were prevalent from before 1862. And the first recorded definition of a Sling, circa 1675 was as follows: "Long-sup or sling was one half water and one half rum with sugar in it to taste."[6]

The use of soda water in Slings is hinted at in 1874: "a drink peculiar to Americans , generally composed of gin, soda-water, ice and slices of lemon." [7]

No Sling recipe yet unearthed between 1675 and 1921, however, contained soda water. Notably, man-made soda water was invented in 1767. And not every permutation of these popular recipes may have found their ways into the primitive print media of their era. Note William Terrington's *Cooling Cups and Dainty Drinks*[8] gives a recipe for Gin and Whisky Slings which don't call for water of any sort, but call for the Sling in a "soda-water glass". Since the origin of the Sling drink form predates the invention of soda water by almost 100 years, recipes may simply have continued to refer to "water." Lacking recipes, the oblique references included here do suggest the use of soda water.

Likewise, Sling recipes published between 1675-1921 contained no pineapple or fruit—or fruit juice other than lemon. In that same period, while no references to such fruit in Slings have been found, such fruits and juices were found in Juleps and Punches—both disparate drink forms of the era—in both recipes and commentary. If these juices were written down when used in Punch, why not in Slings? The answer has to be that the addition was at the very least, uncommon.

---

9. Robert Vermeire, *Cocktails and How to Mix Them* (Jenkins, 1922).

Beyond these primitive origins—to taste the nature of the Slings of the Empire, the British Raj, and the pith-helmeted travelers on holiday in the Orient—one must only turn so far as a bottle of Pimm's #1. A glass, a lump of ice, some Pimm's and a fill of soda water or of ginger ale and the flavor of the late nineteenth-century Sling becomes immediately apparent. It is refreshing, not fruity. It is aromatic, light and slightly piquant—but neither sweet nor rich.

From the evidence presented, the Singapore Sling of today is definitely not a Sling. It has become a "personality drink": a signature libation that is unto itself. But what of the Straits Sling? When did the drink under that original name see print? The earliest-located recipe for the Straits Sling was published in 1922 as written up by Robert Vermeire in *Cocktails and How to Mix Them*. He merely refers to it thusly:

> This well-known Singapore drink, thoroughly ice and shaken, contains:
>
> 2 dashes of Orange Bitters,
> 2 dashes of Angostura Bitters,
> The juice of half a lemon
> One-eighth gill of Bénédictine.
> One-eighth gill of Dry Cherry Brandy
> One-half gill of Gin.
> Pour into a tumbler and fill up with cold soda water.⁹

Superficially, this recipe looks very similar to Singapore Sling recipes that would follow it. While it contains none of the exotic fruit juices that would later be added, it apparently calls for small amounts of two liqueurs. One was traditional and herbal (Benedictine) and one was of fruit (dry cherry brandy.) In the latter case, however, further exploration of the cited book suggests otherwise. The term "dry" in "dry cherry brandy" appears to have been dropped from all subsequent recipe books.

These later publications would either specify cherry brandy or a cherry liqueur. History has given the term "cherry brandy" two meanings. The common one (cherry-flavored brandy liqueur) and the correct one (a clear, unsweetened distillate of cherries.) It is evident to this very day that the term is still being misapplied to the common—and incorrect—meaning. But what, then, did Robert Vermeire mean when he appended the term "dry" to his ingredient? "Dry" hardly describes a liqueur, and if it did describe a cherry liqueur, it would have been the clear and earthy Maraschino. This is evidently not the case, as Vermeire used the term "Maraschino liqueur" freely elsewhere in the book. More likely (almost certain) is that he was making clear he meant real cherry brandy *eau de vie* and not a liqueur.

Since his recipe was the closest in time to the drink's presumed invention, some weight needs to be given to its flavor. And that flavor is remarkably similar to that of the proprietary and secret Pimm's #1 Cup. Its taste is divergent enough to allow it to be a different drink. But as with Pimm's, it is refreshing, not fruity, aromatic, light and piquant—but neither sweet nor rich.

While the earliest published recipe may or may not be the original formulation, it is—in style—more in keeping with the Slings which preceded it than the other recipes offered up as original. The Benedictine added an herbal, gingery character to the drink that is also noted in a Pimm's Cup prepared in the manner of the era. All ingredients in the 1922 recipe were correct and accepted for that drink type up to that time. The other ingredients in purportedly original recipes had not previously been used in Slings before (or shortly after) that time frame.

The flavor of the 1922 version as specified with true cherry brandy eau de vie is much closer to the form of Sling being mixed at the time. Raffles was a British hotel in British Colonial Singapore. Pimm's Cup, Gin & Tonic, as well as refreshers of this sort would appear to be more to the taste of the specified drinker at that time. The use of pineapples and other fruits in drinks seem more connected to the mythical-Polynesian drink craze of the mid-1930s. And that drink type would become popular enough to either radically or incrementally change the recipes and drinking habits of other tropical resort-type areas shortly thereafter as well. This would surely include Singapore.

It appears that the Straits Sling recipe that was invented by Ngiam Tong Boon in 1915—and later lost— was much closer to that in Vermeire's *Cocktails and How to Mix Them* than in later publications or—in fact— what we drink as a Singapore Sling today.

**S**ometime in the past, not only did this drink's name change, but its composition as well— perhaps beginning with a misapprehension about the term "cherry brandy." These were not the only changes, however. Over time, the Singapore Sling transcended its category—and the Sling drink would be dead today without it. Yet, the Singapore Sling ceased to be a Sling a long time ago. Recipe mutations based on the number of years and hands through which the drink went, and the drink's burgeoning status as an icon of a fantasy place contributed to that transcendence. Most of us grew up with a Singapore Sling that was fruity, red, sweet, and festive. Sometimes the true origins of a thing can seem to undermine the underpinnings of what we thought we knew... of a bit of our lives' foundations. Some passion is to be expected. And sometimes tastes just change.

# THE BELLINI

BY LOWELL EDMUNDS

*Who says that ingredients don't make the drink? In the case of the Bellini, the main ingredient—strained white peach pureé—is the difference between bliss and blah. Lowell Edmunds follows the origins of this Italian classic and the time-consuming yet wholly satisfying process it takes to create this warm weather favorite.*

IUSEPPE CIPRIANI, FOUNDER of Harry's Bar, invented the Bellini in 1945, and named it in 1949, after the characteristic rose color in the paintings of Giovanni Bellini (1430-1516).[1] The drink consists of two ingredients, white peach juice and sparkling wine, optionally sweetened with simple syrup.[2] The color of the drink comes from red veins in the pit which attach to the inmost surface of the flesh.

In his history of Harry's Bar, Arrigo "Harry" Cipriani describes his father's invention of the drink:

> Peaches are in abundance throughout Italy from June through September, and my father had a predilection for the white ones. So much so, in fact, that he kept wondering whether there was a way to transform this magic fragrance into a drink which he could offer at Harry's Bar. He experimented by pureéing small white peaches and adding some prosecco (Italian champagne). ...He named it the Bellini, and from that day on the pink champagne drink became part of the Harry's Bar culture. For many years, in the kitchen of Harry's Bar, there were those whose sole function was to create the pureé by actually squeezing and pitting the small and fragrant fruit with their hands. ...But because we depended on the peach season for fresh fruit, we could make the Bellini only during these four months.[3]

---

1. My dates for the drink come from Caumo 1999: 26. Cipriani 1996: 87-88, however, gives 1948. The account of the Bellini in Cipriani 1996 is practically the same as the one in Cipriani 2000: 16-17.

2. On simple syrup, which turns out to be a less simple subject than one ever suspected, see Darcy S. O'Neal in this volume. With all due (and heart-felt) respect to Dale DeGroff, the traditional Bellini does not contain peach liqueur (cf. DeGroff 2002: 80).

3. Cipriani 1996: 87.

The drink was so closely identified with the bar that Harry imagined his father drinking Bellinis in heaven.[4] He named his second restaurant in New York "Bellini" (opened 1987).

The drink is simple but elusive. It is almost impossible to find the real thing in a bar. It is a labor-intensive, do-it-yourself project, the time for which someone else chooses. That someone is nature, and the time is summer, and, within summer, the moment when ripe white peaches arrive in the farmers market. No one in his or her right mind drinks a Bellini in wintertime, even if frozen peach pureé makes it possible to defy nature. The Bellini is one of the fleeting joys of summer. What about its place in the day? The Bellini is too heavy to function as an aperitif before lunch or dinner. Moving back to the beginning of the day, it goes well, like orange juice and champagne, at breakfast. Or, moving to the opposite end, after dinner, it could go with dessert. I dream of a white peach triple: tart, sorbet, and Bellini.

The drink is simple but arduous to prepare. The peach juice challenges everyone, amateur and professional, neither of whom has someone in the kitchen exclusively devoted to pitting and squeezing peaches. A food mill or juicer helps, up to a point. It produces pureé. The pureé is then hand-pressed through a sieve or cheesecloth. (This crucial step is omitted in all of the recipes I have seen on web pages.) If the pureé is too thick to work with, add a little of the sparkling wine. In this case, the results of the pressing will then be a crude Bellini, awaiting adjustment of proportions and sweetness, the two main variables. But ideally one has come home from the farmers market with peaches just on the verge of ripeness, which will lend themselves to pressing.[5]

---

4. Cipriani 1996: ch. 3 "("Bellinis in Paradise").

The bartender can order frozen pureé from The Perfect Pureé of Napa Valley, which has an impressive web page.[6] The unit is a case of six 30-ounce jars. Sugar is added (Brix: 20-22), as are citric and ascorbic acids, as a preservative. The description of the product specifies white peaches and speaks of a "blush" produced by the red veins. It sounds promising, but, as I have already indicated, I am pessimistic about the chances of producing anything like the classic Bellini from frozen pureé.

How sweet should the Bellini be? Sweet enough to express the flavor of the peaches—"*un gusto amabile*," in the words Ruggero "Roger" Caumo, who was the head barman at Harry's Bar from the late 1940s until 1983. Lemon juice has, however, found its way into recipes for this drink. Where did this idea come from? Perhaps from some misunderstood tradition going back to Harry's Bar itself. Caumo, in the recipe he gives in his memoir, calls for lemon juice in the ratio of 1:10 in order to prevent oxidation of the peach juice. His recipe is for a batch of ten drinks, and he no doubt imagines the juice sitting around for some period of time or going into and out of a refrigerator.[7]

The proportions are partly a matter of taste, partly determined by the two main ingredients. In a highly standardized bar operation, employing the frozen pureé mentioned above, one could know the proportion in advance and simply crank out the Bellinis. At home, it will be different each time. No matter how fine the juice, the drink is going to be thick, and one is searching for a compromise between liquidity and expression of the peaches.[8]

The other variables are color and coldness. If the peaches do not produce the desirable pink color, one can

---

5. There is an old wives' tale that if you put peaches in a paper bag it will speed their ripening. I have not experimented with this technique.

6. http://www.perfectpuree.com/pp/index.php. Accessed 12/7/04.

7. To tell the truth, I do not know what the relation between oxidation and temperature is, i.e. if refrigeration retards oxidation. Darcy O'Neal to the rescue!

add the juice of a few raspberries or cherries. Ruggero "Roger" Caumo authorizes this subterfuge. The recipe in *The Harry's Bar Cookbook* stresses coldness. It depends on the ambient temperature. One seeks the magic ratio between it and the temperature of the drink. On a very hot day, chill everything. If it is 70° F, only the wine has to be chilled.

As for the choice of sparkling wine, as in the quotation from Cipriani above, it was originally prosecco, and, to the taste of the present writer, this wine produces the right degree of effervescence in the drink and the right flavor. Asti Spumante is, to the same taste, very sweet, and works well with tart peach juice. Champagne is also possible, which should be sec, not brut. By tasting the two ingredients separately, you can sense what the proportions should be, and you will not have to waste peach juice on experiments.

Finally, what kind of glass? Caumo calls for a flute. In the beautiful photograph in *The Harry's Bar Cookbook*, it is not a flute but a kind of tumbler with a fairly thick bottom. I have not had a Bellini in Harry's Bar since 1956, when Venice was already becoming croweded in the summer, but I remember that it was served in a cylindrical glass about four or five inches tall and of modest diameter.

## ANNOTATED BIBLIOGRAPHY:

Caley, Nora. "Bella Bellini." Search for this article by name on Google. (The web address is long.) Describes the

---

8. As for the last of these, *The Harry's Bar Cookbook* just mentioned calls for 1 part peach juice to 3 parts wine, Caumo for 1 to 2. The decision depends partly on whether the peach element is closer to purée or to juice. The difference here is perhaps generational, or perhaps a matter of the peach juice which Caumo had available to him, i.e., one can imagine a decline in this particular material, along with other aspects of the decline of Harry's Bar.

Bellini in the current bar scene in the U.S., with some truly horrendous recipes.

Caumo, Ruggero. 1999. *Ricordi del barman Ruggero all'Harry's Bar*. Treviso: Vin Veneto, 1999.

Cipriani, Arrigo. 1986. *Eloisa e il Bellini: Romanzo*. Milan: Longanesi. Trans.: Cipriani 1991. For a summary go to www.cipriani.com/cipriani/Gifts/Books/books3.htm. Accessed 12/13/04.

_____ . (Harry). 1991. *Heloise and Bellinis*. Trans. by Ronald Strom. New York: Arcade. Translation of Cipriani 1986. I have read neither the translation nor the original.

_____. 1996. *The Harry's Bar: The Life and Times of the Legendary Venice Landmark*. New York: Arcade.

_____. 1997. *La leggenda dell'Harry's bar*. Milano: Sperling and Kupfer. I have not seen it. No doubt it is the Italian version of Cipriani 1996. I remember that in 1991 there was a book about the bar by Cipriani on sale at Harry's Bar in Venice. Are Cipriani 1996 and 1997 re-pottings of that book?

_____. 2000. *The Harry's Bar Cookbook*. London: Blake.

DeGroff, Dale. 2002. *The Craft of the Cocktail*. New York: Clarkson Potter.

# IF YOU LIKE PIÑA COLADAS

## THE HISTORY OF THE PIÑA COLDA

### BY JARED BROWN

*Cocktails are among history's bastard children, acknowledged years after their birth, and then only if they reach prominence. Once a Cocktail achieves notoriety, people begin to wonder who its parent is. But anyone who pursues this truth inevitably faces a dearth of information about the Cocktail's infancy. Yet Cocktails—each as products of their time—can speak volumes for themselves if we look hard enough. Most can be traced to the actions of an imaginative bartender or passionate amateur, the fads of an era and the tastes of a region. However, after delving into the birth of the most broadly influential Cocktail of all time, Jared Brown shows readers that the Piña Colada's history would be incomplete without a look at two other inventions: the electric blender and processed cream of coconut.*

**J**AMES BOND NEVER ORDERED ONE. It's hard to picture Hemingway setting a frosty one down next to his typewriter. It's the drink of choice for countless cruise ship passengers and sunburned Florida tourists sporting loud Hawaiian shirts. With the later additions of the umbrella and cherry garnish, in a Martini drinking world the Piña Colada has even come to symbolize this crowd. The Internet Cocktail Database goes so far as to define all "blender drinks" as "thick, festive, and dessert-like potions popular among infrequent drinkers."[1]

However, as this article will seek to prove, the Piña Colada is the most broadly influential Cocktail ever created, and is worthy of a place beside such vaunted tropical libations as the Mojito and Daiquiri. First, the matter of who invented the Piña Colada needs to be settled. Like Kurosawa's classic film *Rashomon*, there are three plausible but conflicting stories of three inventors: Ramón "Monchito" Marrero Pérez, Ricardo Gracia and Ramón Mingot. Thankfully, one is easy to eliminate. The other two arrive complete with supporting evidence and eyewitness reports. Here, the facts will be laid out without judgment.

## BIRTH AT THE CARIBE HILTON

**I**t is generally accepted that the Piña Colada was introduced in Puerto Rico, in the Caribe Hilton's Beachcomber Bar on August 15, 1954.[2] The resort was still relatively new. Opened on December 9, 1949, it was the first hotel in San Juan to feature such mod-

---

1. Internet Cocktail Database at www.cocktaildb.com/barwr_detail?id-100.
2. "Caribe Hilton, Birthplace of the Piña Colada, Celebrates the Cocktail's 50th Anniversary" Press release issued by the Caribe Hilton. Year confirmed through interviews with former Caribe Hilton staff. This has been variously reported as 1957.

ern luxuries as individual push-button air conditioners in every room, and a telephone and radio in every cabaña. Thirty planeloads of furniture were airlifted to Puerto Rico for the hotel in a joint effort with Pan-Am and Eastern Airlines dubbed the "largest single commercial air movement of freight".[3]

With its prime beachfront location and amenities, the hotel drew an affluent, international clientele. By 1954, it was a popular celebrity destination. John Wayne, Elizabeth Taylor, Charleton Heston, Ray Milland, Joan Collins, José Ferrar and Gloria Swanson stayed there.[4] Joan Crawford even declared the Caribe Hilton's Piña Colada was "better than slapping Bette Davis in the face."[5] (It's no surprise the Beachcomber's Cocktails were praised from the start. Hilton Hotels brought in experienced barmen from New York's Plaza Hotel and the Waldorf-Astoria to set up the bars and train the bartenders.)[6]

### CARIBE HILTON'S PIÑA COLADA
In a blender, combine:
2 ounces white rum
I ounce coconut cream
I ounce heavy cream
6 ounces fresh pineapple juice
I half cup crushed ice

Blend until smooth, about 15 seconds. Garnish with pineapple wedge and marachino cherry.[7]

3. "Caribe Hilton Celebrates 50 Glamorous Years on December 9" Press release issued by the Caribe Hilton.
4. "Caribe Hilton 50th Anniversary" promotional card from 2004, commemorating the Piña Colada's anniversary.
5. See "Birth of the Piña Colada" www.frommers.com/destinations/sanjuan/0323027721.html
6. Telephone interview with Hector Torres, March 18, 2005.
7. "Caribe Hilton 50th Anniversary" promotional card from 2004, commemorating the Piña Colada's anniversary.

The bar scene at the Caribe Hilton's Beachcomber Bar when it first opened in the mid-1950s. (Photo courtesy of the Caribe Hilton.)

One of the hotel's early local bartenders, Ramón "Monchito"[8] Marrero Pérez from Aguas Buenas, PR, has been credited with the Piña Colada's invention for five decades by the Caribe Hilton. As cited in numerous hotel press releases and promotional materials as well as articles written about the hotel and the Piña Colada, Monchito is said to have spent three months experimenting before he finally created a Cocktail he felt captured "the sunny, tropical flavor of Puerto Rico in a glass."[9]

Another Caribe Hilton barman, Ricardo Gracia, has been quoted in numerous articles, claiming that he invented the Piña Colada. Gracia, who joined Hilton Hotels in Spain in 1951, worked in a number of beverage operations positions at the Caribe Hilton from approximately 1952 to 1970, before moving on to other venues in the chain. He retired from Hilton in 1986. A year later he became sommelier—and resident Piña Colada and sangria expert—in the Augustine Grill at the Sawgrass Marriott Hotel in Ponte Verde Beach, FL, until his next retirement at age 90 on September 15, 2004.[10] (Vinnie Dagostino, the Sawgrass Marriott's food and beverage manager who credits Gracia for much of his wine training, said the resort continues to make Piña Coladas and sangria per Gracia's specifications.)[11]

In a 2005 interview published in *Coastal Living*,[12] Gracia explained that he was making another of his creations—the Coco Loco (rum, coconut cream, and crushed ice served

---

8. Monchito was also called "Moncho" by his friends, according to Norman Parkhurst, former manufacturer of Coco López.

9. "Caribe Hilton 50th Anniversary" promotional card from 2004, commemorating the Piña Colada's anniversary.

10. Jim Bragg, "The Piña Colada—a Flavorful History", Cruisemates, September 16, 2000, cruisemates.com/articles/humop/pinacoloda.cfm

11. Telephone interview with Vinnie Dagostino, March 21, 2005.

12. Judy Alexandra Diedwardo, "Coastal Character: Ricardo Gracia," *Coastal Living*, Mar 2005.

in a hulled-out coconut)[13]—as a welcome Cocktail for the Caribe Hilton's guests. One day, the pickers who gathered coconuts from the trees around the resort went on strike. Gracia noticed that the hotel had received a large shipment of pineapples. Rather than serve his Cocktails in glasses, he hollowed out pineapples and served his Coco Locos in them. He loved the pineapple flavor and accentuated it by adding pineapple juice. Then he named the drink for the strained pineapple he added. Literally translated, Piña Colada means "strained pineapple".

According to Gracia, here's the original recipe:

### PIÑA COLADA
One fresh pineapple
One green coconut
White Rum
One cup crushed ice

Pour the juice of the coconut into blender. Add a scoop of the coconut's jelly. Chop off the top of the pineapple and set aside. Hollow out the pineapple using a pineapple cutter and place contents in blender. Mix pineapple and coconut well. Add the rum. Add crushed ice and blend five minutes until creamy. (In Gracia's words: "It's very important that it's creamy. Some bartenders add too much ice and it becomes a sorbet. It's not a frozen drink. If it's frozen, it's nothing. Creamy, creamy!")[14] Pour Piña Colada into the hollowed out pineapple. Make a hole in the top of the pineapple for a straw, close and serve.[15]

Hector Torres, of Gurabo, PR, joined the Caribe Hilton in 1952. There, he worked with Monchito and Ricardo Gracia, first preparing the bartenders' garnishes and stocking the wells as a bar back (they were called bar boys at that time); then making drinks himself as a bartender.

---

13. This drink is not the same as the Dominican Coco Loco made with amaretto, coconut cream, grenadine, milk, pineapple juice and light rum; or the Coco Loco made in Mexico, which combines Coco López, grenadine, tequila, vodka, gin and rum.

14. Phone interview with Ricardo Gracia, March 21, 2005.

15. Gary Smith, "Profile: Of Kindred Spirits," *T&L Golf*, Mar/Apr 1998, p. 142.

When asked who invented the Piña Colada, there was no hesitation in his voice, "Monchito!"[16]

According to Torres, Gracia was his and Monchito's supervisor. As such, Gracia was undoubtedly present at the Piña Colada's birth, likely influencing or participating in its invention and early promotion. However, Torres was not the only surviving witness to dispute Gracia's claim to be the drink's sole inventor.

Miguel Marquez, who worked as a waiter, head waiter and maitre'd at the Caribe Hilton from 1951 to 1998, remembered working with Monchito, Torres and Gracia. In a phone interview, Marquez also said Monchito invented the Piña Colada, additionally stating that at the time, Torres had already taken Gracia's place as Monchito's supervisor.[17]

Marquez agreed with Torres that most of the early Piña Coladas were served in tall glasses, garnished with a pine-apple slice. However, he pointed out that some were served inside pineapples or coconuts as a photo of Monchito shows. Score one point for Gracia.

Torres also remembered the Coco Loco that Gracia mentioned in the Coastal Living interview, though he recalled making it with rum, apricot brandy, coconut water and a little Coco López. According to him, the mixture was shaken vigorously and strained into a coconut.[18]

## BIRTH AT BARRACHINA

plaque on the arched entry of the Barrachina Restaurant in Old San Juan proclaims that Ramón Portas Mingot invented the Piña

---

16. Phone interview with Ramón Torres, March 16, 2005.
17. Phone interview with Miguel Marquez, March 17, 2005.
18. Phone interview with Ramón Torres, March 18, 2005.

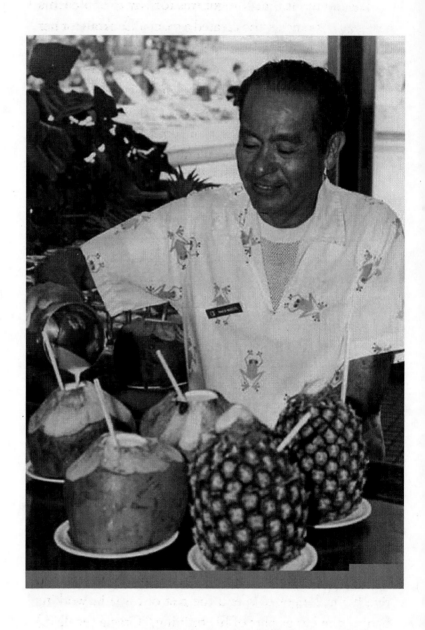

Ramón "Monchito" Marrero Pérez serving up Piña Coladas in both pineapples and coconuts at the Caribe Hilton's Beachcomber Bar. (Photo courtesy of Caribe Hilton.)

Colada there in 1963: *"La casa donde nacio la piña colada en el ano 1963 por Don Ramón Portas Mingot."*[19]

Legend has it that Mingot was too shy to approach a beautiful customer, so he created a special Cocktail for her based on improving, even perfecting a combination of pineapple, coconut, and rum that farmers and fishermen had enjoyed for some time. She became his wife, and true to all legends they lived happily ever after.

But eyewitness accounts from Torres and Marquez date the Piña Colada's birth and naming in 1954, nine years before Mingot mixed his love potion at Barrachina. Still, Barrachina's classic seventeenth-century courtyard bar and restaurant that specializes in native Puerto Rican dishes is worth a visit. Plus its Piña Coladas are excellent.

I reached Ricardo Gracia on his ranch in St. Augustine, FL, and asked him if he could set the record straight. Gracia explained that he had worked in Spain, starting out in his parent's Barcelona restaurant and finally owning two of the city's finest restaurants, Saratoga and Arizona. In 1951, he sold his establishments and accepted an invitation to join Hilton Hotels. After a year as bar manager at the Hilton Castellana in Madrid, Gracia was transferred to the Caribe Hilton—with one major detour. En route to San Juan, he spent a month in New York working and being trained behind the bars at the Plaza, Waldorf-Astoria, Roosevelt, and New Yorker hotels.

As the Caribe Hilton's bar manager, he remembered Torres and a bar back named Carlos whose primary job was to squeeze the fresh orange, pineapple, grapefruit and lemon juices for all of the bars. ("If he finished in less than five hours, he got to spend the rest of his shift working behind the bar as part of his training," Gracia recalled.)

---

19. Karibik Reisin, Puerto Rico - Geburtsort der Piña Colada, www.touristik-links.de/reisen-466.html

He also remembered Monchito as the bartender who made coconut cream for him, which he used in his Coco Locos.

When asked who invented the Piña Colada, Gracia replied chivalrously, "We did. Monchito, me, Hector Torres, Carlos, Roger Lopéz, Enrique. We did. The Caribe Hilton crew was like a family. You want to know who invented the Piña Colada? Just remember one name: The Caribe Hilton."

In the 1960s, Gracia traveled extensively in Europe for the Hilton Corporation, training bartenders, giving seminars and making public appearances. He visited Rome, Venice, Provence, Valencia and Paris. In London he demonstrated the Piña Colada for the International Bartenders Guild and on BBC television.[20]

As for the Barrachina's claim, Gracia said, "The bartender there worked for me at the Caribe Hilton before he worked at Barrachina."

## COCO LÓPEZ

One claim frequently ignored by most Cocktail authorities is that the first Piña Colada was made with Coco López. This statement appears to be true. In fact, it is not strong enough. Certainly, the modern Piña Colada would not have been invented, much less widely adopted, if not for pre-made cream of coconut.

Where did Coco López come from? In the late 1940s, the Universidad de Puerto Rico (Puerto Rico University) received a research and development grant from the Puerto Rican government to promote new industry for the island commonwealth.[21] A professor of agriculture and/or chem-

---

20. Phone interview with Ricardo Gracia, March 21, 2005.

istry during the early 1950s, Don Ramón López-Irizarry received some of these funds to forward his research on the extraction of cream from coconut meat.[22]

Coconut cream was a common cooking ingredient throughout the tropics, but it was very labor intensive to prepare. Try it for yourself, using Dora Romano's recipes for *coco rallado* (grated coconut) and *leche de coco* (coconut milk) from her book *Rice and Beans and Tasty Things:*[23]

### GRATED COCONUT
#### (Coco rallado)

Shake the coconut to make sure that it is full of water, and thus still fresh. Pierce two of the eyelets of the coconut with a pointed tool or ice pick. Drain the liquid and save for other purposes. (It is a very refreshing drink chilled in the icebox.) Break the coconut open by hitting it with a hammer about its widest part. Break into smaller pieces. Remove the meat from the shell by prying it out with a strong short knife, such as an oyster knife. Pare the brown skin next to the meat with a paring knife, vegetable peeler, or scrape it off with a hand grater. Cut the meat into 1-inch pieces. On a food processor fitted with a steel blade, process in small batches until it is well grated, or grate with a hand grater.

### COCONUT MILK
#### (Leche de coco)

Grate de coconut [sic] and measure, p. 415 (*see above*). Add half the amount of water as grated coconut. Squeeze through a clean cloth kitchen napkin by small portions. Measure this heavy milk. Determine how much more milk your recipe asks for, if any. Measure that amount in water and add to the already squeezed coconut. Squeeze again as in step 3. Add this milk to the heavy milk already measured to reach that amount needed. Proceed with your recipe.

---

21. See Irizarry at www.searchspaniel.com/index.php/Ramon_López_Irizarry
22. Ibid.
23. Dora Romano, *Rice and Beans and Tasty Things* (San Juan, PR: A Puerto Rican Cookbook, 1986) pp. 415-416.

[ED. NOTE: Some recipes use the reserved coconut water in place of a portion of tap or spring water.]

You then allow the coconut milk to settle for a few hours before skimming the desired coconut cream off the top.

Irizarry automated this arduous task. Using industrial graters, presses and multiple pressings, and a centrifuge separation process, he developed efficient ways to extract coconut cream. After the cream was pressed and separated, he sweetened it with cane sugar.

He started selling Coco López in 1954. Irizarry began by personally approaching bartenders and chefs around San Juan, encouraging them to experiment with his new creation. He saw Coco López as an essential ingredient for coquitos (a traditional Puerto Rican holiday drink similar to egg nog) and for baking.

Torres fondly remembered meeting him at the Caribe Hilton on several occasions. He said Coco López representative came there because he wanted the hotel to try his new product. Torres stated that the bartenders used Coco López to create the first Piña Coladas.[24] He was also fairly certain that the Caribe Hilton was among Irizarry's first customers, possibly the first.

Gracia remembers giving Irizarry samples of the coconut cream that Monchito was making, and said that Irizarry based Coco López on Gracia's recipe for coconut cream.

Enter Norman Parkhurst.

When Irizarry started out, he had a small plant where he could produce 15 to 20 cases of product per day: equivalent to about 300 coconuts.[25] He trucked the finished cream of coconut to a canning facility about a mile away. The Parkhurst family had a canning factory nearby, where

---

24. Interview with Ramón Torres, March 18, 2005.

Over the decades, Coco López's packaging has changed very little. The can in the upper left is from the old Bayamón, PR facility. And all the packages feature a Piña Colada recipe that uses three ounces of rum. (Photo by Jared Brown.)

they produced canned fruit juices. Their professional relationship with Irizarry began in the 1960s when Irizarry was considering retirement and asked if they would be interested in buying him out. They had a better idea. They would buy the cream of coconut from him, package it and promote it.

Parkhurst suspects it was not Irizarry that Torres and Gracia met. "He never touched a drop of alcohol. He never thought about using Coco López in a Cocktail. I don't think he was ever in a bar or nightclub in his life. He was a chemist who lectured at the university for many years."[26]

Most histories of Irizarry claim that he left the university to start Coco López. He may have been connected to the university as late as 1970, when the school ordered and received a Vincent VP-6 industrial press. According to Vincent Presses, this particular model was sent to Irizarry for the production of Coco López.[27] The press would have likely gone to the university's agricultural experiment station (Estacion Experimental Agricola).

Coco López, of course, has been promoting its own recipe in its promotional literature for over thirty years:

### RECIPE FOR THE PERFECT PIÑA COLADA
In an electric blender combine:
2 ounces Coco López
1.5 ounces Puerto Rican rum
2 ounces unsweetened pineapple juice.

Add about 6 ounces (two-thirds of a glass) of cracked ice. Blend for 30 seconds. Serve in a tall glass. If you want to go all the way, garnish with a pineapple stick and top with a maraschino cherry.[28]

---

25. A product sell sheet from Coco López.
26. Phone interview with Norman Parkhurst, March 23, 2005.
27. See www.vincentcorp.com/products/issue31.html. According to the same release, by 1995, Vincent Corporation had added large VP-16 presses for the first pressing, and smaller VP-12's and 10's for the second and third pressings. A rotating cone option was added on to maximize yield.

The first Piña Coladas were not all made in an electric blender. During the mid-1950s, the Caribe Hilton employed 49 bar employees and three or four electric blenders, according to Hector Torres. He related the following as the original recipe and method of preparation if a blender was not available:

### PIÑA COLADA
A cup of shaved ice
4 ounces pineapple juice
1.5 ounces white rum[29]
2 ounces coconut cream

Combine all ingredients in a shaker. Shake well. Strain the mixture into a frozen 14-ounce Collins glass. Then add the shaved ice directly from the shaker. Garnish with a chunk of fresh pineapple.

The hotel did not immediately add more electric blenders when the Piña Colada was invented. As Torres explained, "It wasn't a popular drink when it was first introduced. No one had heard of it. Monchito would make up batches and pour them into three-ounce glasses. Then he would give these away to customers. When they finished, they would usually order a Piña Colada. He worked hard to introduce people to Piña Coladas. We all did."

Miguel Marquez said that Monchito and other staff members would encourage departing customers to remember to order Piña Coladas whenever they returned to Puerto Rico.[30]

---

28. "The Story of Coco López: Once upon a time there was no Piña Colada," a promotional sheet created by Coco López Imports, 1977.

29. According to Hector Torres and Ricardo Gracia, the original rum was Ron Rico, which at the time was made in Puerto Rico. The Caribe Hilton switched to Don Q white rum, then to Bacardi in the early 1960s after Bacardi relocated from Cuba to Cataño, PR, across the bay from Old San Juan.

Parkhurst verified that the barmen actively promoted the Piña Colada. In fact, it was the Parkhursts who initiated this promotion. Two nights a week, Coco López hired a piano player to perform at the Beachcomber Bar, while the bartenders made complimentary Piña Coladas for the guests. When they saw that the home blenders used in the hotel were constantly breaking down, they bought commercial blenders and loaned them to the bar. Parkhurst did not remember Gracia, but considered "Moncho"[31] to be a very close friend, and hailed him as the Piña Colada's inventor.

The Caribe Hilton promotion was so successful that Coco López began moving their entertainer to other San Juan hotels and bars. Then they added another promotional tool to tie-in with their Piña Colada nights: a Piña Colada kit.

The kit contained two tall frosted glasses, Coco López, pineapple juice, printed napkins and recipe cards. The kits sold for four or five dollars in hotel gift shops and souvenir stores, paired with Bacardi Rum. Coco López started out producing a few hundred kits a week, but the demand skyrocketed. Barrachina, a popular tourist destination, sold a truckload of these kits each week for ten dollars, according to Parkhurst.

Good fortune and good business sense helped the Parkhursts overcome two limitations around this time. Originally, Irizarry's daughter created the batches of Coco López in their plant, and shipped the finished product to the cannery to safeguard the recipe as a trade secret. She was incapable of producing more than 500 cases a month. This was not nearly enough to keep up with the Parkhurst's successful advertising and promotion campaign.

---

30. Phone interview with Miguel Marquez, March 17, 2005.
31. Also known as "Monchito."

Finally they managed to buy Irizarry out and expanded the production facilities.

Then David Ballachow, a tourist visiting Puerto Rico with his business partner, tried his first Piña Colada and was hooked. He sought out the Parkhursts and forged a deal to import and sell Coco López in the United States, where it was only sold in a few of New York's Hispanic specialty stores. Starting in his home state of Maryland, Ballachow's company managed to set up a nationwide distribution network.

Back in San Juan, it didn't take long for the Piña Colada to catch on at the Caribe Hilton, or for the hotel to add blenders. Today, the Piña Colada is the resort's most popular Cocktail, and there are definitely enough blenders to handle the demand.

## THE ELECTRIC BLENDER

**N**early all Piña Coladas are now made in electric blenders. Though the blender was invented before the Piña Colada, its rise in popularity, like that of Coco López, runs roughly parallel to the Piña Colada.

Steven Poplawski was the owner of The Stevens Electric Company, located in Racine, WI. Poplawski invented the electric blender, in 1922, to overcome the challenge of blending Horlick's Malted Milk—another innovation created at Racine—into milkshakes in soda fountains. (Racine was a hotbed of invention around the turn of the nineteenth century and takes credit for such timesavers as Johnson's Wax, the electric floor polisher, the portable vacuum cleaner, the lawn mower and the automobile.)[32]

Poplawski's creation—the first to position a spinning blade in the base of the blender cup—had a number of major flaws. For one, it's said that it leaked like a sieve straight onto the electric motor.

It wasn't until 1937, when Fred Waring (who purchased the design from Fred Osius who had purchased it from Steven Poplawski) introduced an improved version at the National Restaurant Show in Chicago that the blender first came to the attention of the public.

Fred Waring was bandleader of The Pennsylvanians for nearly seven decades. So most people know this Congressional Gold Medal recipient as "The Man Who Taught America to Sing". However, Fred Waring was also a tireless promoter of his blender, which he named the Waring Mixer. There are countless stories of him showing up at department stores or making blended drinks for the press. At one point he even changed his group's name to The Blendors (his preferred spelling).

He was also adept at recruiting friends to help. According to Virginia Waring, his widow, Waring's first recruit was Rudy Vallee. He invited the crooner into his dressing room, knowing that Vallee loved frozen Daiquiris. He made him a blended Strawberry Daiquiri (which Waring later claimed he personally invented). Vallee liked it so much he asked to become Waring's first salesman, and left with a blender of his own. Vallee then walked into bars as he toured across the country. If he didn't see a blender, he'd order a frozen Daiquiri and ask the bartender if he had a blender. If he didn't, Vallee would pull one out and demonstrate it. If the bar had one, he'd simply ask the bartender about it as if he'd never seen one before, and then ask to try a frozen Daiquiri. Either way, the bartender or bar owner

---

32. See the "Birth of the Blender," www.egullet.org/index.cgi?pg=ARTICLE-blender

would frequently insist on ordering an extra blender for Vallee. By his estimate, he received around 350, which he gave away to friends.[33]

World War II slowed the manufacture and sales of all consumer appliances, but the booming post-war western economy more than compensated for its slow start. In 1946, John Oster had purchased The Stevens Electric Company and launched the Osterizer. Despite this new competition, in 1954—the same year the Piña Colada was invented—Fred Waring celebrated the sale of his millionth blender.[34]

Consumers were now equipped for and receptive to blender Cocktails. Waring once boasted with uncanny foresight about his blender to a St. Louis reporter, "…this mixer is going to revolutionize American drinks."

## THE SONG THAT SOLD A MILLION COCKTAILS

The brightest musical spotlight that ever fell on the Piña Colada was Rupert Holmes' infectious love song "Escape (The Pina Colada Song)" from his *Partners in Crime* album that hit number one on the US music charts in December, 1979, and January, 1980.[35] This tune cemented the Piña Colada's position in the minds of a generation of young Americans as the ultimate casual, decadent, romantic indulgence. (As the lyrics say, "if you're not into health food.") Those twenty- to forty-somethings, interestingly, are now the forty- to sixty-somethings, who make up the bulk of the cruise ship business.

33. Virginia Waring, Fred Waring and the Pennsylvanians, University of Illinois Press, Champaign, IL, 1997.

34. Mary Bellis, "The Blender—the History of the Kitchen Blender", at inventors.about.com/library/inventors/blblender.htm

35. A history of the song appears at www.songfacts.com/detail.lasso?id=2896.

Holmes admitted that he had never tried a Piña Colada before he wrote and recorded the song. In fact, his original lyric had been "If you like Humphrey Bogart", not "If you like Piña Coladas". He felt that he'd used movie references in enough songs, so he considered using a drink instead. Holmes recalled his moment of inspiration, "When you go on vacation to the islands, when you sit on the beach and someone asks you if you'd like a drink, you never order a Budweiser, you don't have a beer. You're on vacation, you want a drink in a hollowed out pineapple with the flags of all nations and a long straw. I thought, 'Let's see, there's Daiquiri, Mai Tai, Piña Colada—I wonder what a Piña Colada tastes like...'"[36]

This was the last song recorded for the album, and Holmes wrote the lyrics the night before the recording session. He sang the song beginning to end in the morning when he arrived at the recording studio. This recording was to be a "scratch track" for the lead guitarist to work from. In subsequent recordings Holmes could not match the spontaneity and energy of that recording, so the final vocals on the album were recorded the first time he ever sang the song.

The song started with the working title "People Need Other People" and was originally released on the Infinity/MCA record label as "Escape." The record company added the parenthetical subtitle later because people were calling radio stations requesting "the Piña Colada song". MCA was losing record sales because of the confusion.

If Holmes had never tried a Piña Colada, how did it come to mind? One possible source is Warren Zevon's May 1978 hit "Werewolves of London", which included the line "I saw a werewolf drinking a Piña Colada at Trader Vic's/His hair was perfect."

---

35. A history of the song appears at www.songfacts.com/detail.lasso?id=2896.

## A COCKTAIL GAINS LEGITIMACY

The year 1978 was a landmark for the Piña Colada outside the music studios, too. On July 17, 1978, Governor Rafael Hernandez Colon of Puerto Rico issued a public proclamation, making the Piña Colada the national drink of Puerto Rico. Monchito attended the ceremony, as did representatives of Coco López, including Norman Parkhurst, who presented him with a color television set as a token of their gratitude.

## SO WHAT'S IN A NAME?

Is the Piña Colada the most influential cocktail ever made? The Martini has spawned an entire category of drinks. Just as the word Kleenex® started as a brand name and became a generic term for facial tissues and "Cocktail" went from describing a drink with liquor, sugar, water and bitters to enveloping nearly all spirituous drinks, "Martini" is now commonly used to describe nearly any strong drink served in a cocktail glass. The Cocktail glass itself is now also known as a Martini glass.

Similarly, the Colada suffix has become a Cocktail term denoting a frozen drink made with cream of coconut and usually rum. For example, there's the Strawberry Colada, Banana Colada, Strawberry-Banana Colada, Kahlua Colada, Bailey's Colada, Nutty Colada, Mango-Melon Colada, Kiwi Colada, and so on. There are quite a few, but there is no question that the Martini has spawned more eponymous drinks.

If a Cocktail's influence is measured by the extent to which its flavor and aroma have been replicated outside of Cocktails, however, the Piña Colada rises above all other beverages—alcoholic or not. Piña Colada appears in incense, candles, soaps, shampoos, air fresheners, moisturizers, ice cream, sorbet, Lifesavers®, lollipops, jelly beans, weight loss and bodybuilding supplements, cosmetics, soft drinks, herbal tea, popcorn, peanut butter, scented bowling balls, medications (human and veterinary), saxophone reeds, and pipe tobacco. This is just a brief sampling. Its prevalence as a flavor in the adult-products industry (personal lubricants, warming oils, whipped body toppings, etc.) points to its broadly perceived sensuality. No other drink can claim such broad recognition.

It would be easy to dismiss this profusion of Piña Colada flavor, scent and Cocktail variation as coincidental to the drink itself since the combination of pineapple and coconut is not new or rare. Pineapples are native to Puerto Rico (called *yayama* by the Taino Indians) as well as to much of Central America and South America as far down as Brazil. Long before 1954, pineapples were farmed commercially as far away as Australia and Thailand. Coconuts are abundant in all of these areas, and plenty of recipes combining these flavors predate the mid-1950s advent of the Piña Colada.

However, the phrase "Piña Colada" does not translate to "pineapple coconut," but as mentioned earlier, literally means "strained pineapple".[37] Through this misnomer, it is clear that any combination of pineapple and coconut—either in scent or flavor—that's named Piña Colada, or any reference to the presence of coconut by using the "Colada" suffix draws directly from the Cocktail not from coincidence.

---

37. In many interviews, Gracia said the name came about when he strained pineapple juice into his Coco Loco. In a phone interview, Torres said the name referred to using the blender or vigorously shaking and then straining the drink before adding the ice from the shaker into the glass. Parkhurst thought Monchito might have been referring to the straining process involved in making cream of coconut.

There may never be a precise answer as to who invented the Piña Colada. Was it Monchito? Gracia? Monchito and Gracia?

Regardless, there are some certainties. It was invented at the Caribe Hilton, though the recipe touted by the resort is not the original (everyone agrees the marachino cherry much was a later addition, and some question the heavy cream). There is no question that the Coco López Company was and is the Piña Colada's greatest proponent, and that it rode the proliferation of the blender into bars around the world.

In its first 50 years, this drink rose from inspiration to regional specialty, to become one of the most ubiquitous resort Cocktails. Beyond that, it has spawned an entire category of scent and taste, and has become an icon of a generation that likes Piña Coladas, even if they don't really like getting caught in the rain.

*There's more to a Cocktail than ingredients and execution. Often, the life of its inventor is just as compelling as the drink itself. The history of a particular spirit sometimes finds itself enmeshed with the chronicles of a nation's history. The research involved in the writing of a book on drinks and spirits can lead the author down unknown paths of literary exploration. The making of a component as basic as simple syrup can embody more science than most people ever assume. And the challenge to create new recipes can lead to new adventures in the kitchen to discover new techniques...*

# AND OTHER THINGS

# ANTOINE AMEDEE PEYCHAUD

## PHARMACIST AND NEW ORLEANS COCKTAIL LEGEND

BY PHIL GREENE

*As enigmatic as the origins of the classics themselves, myths and legends have built up around the term "Cocktail" itself.*
*H.L. Mencken's traced of the wood's etymology to a number of divergent sources. And although authorities agree that the term first appeared in print in an upstate New York newspaper in 1806, the person most associated with the word "Cocktail" was a nineteenth-century New Orleans pharmacist—Antoine Amedee Peychaud. Phil Greene, a Peychaud descendant, dug deep into the records to find out more about his ancestor, who created Peychaud's Aromatic Cocktail Bitters—a prime ingredient in the first of the great New Orleans Cocktails, the Sazerac.*

# IT'S THE BITTER TRUTH

### Peychaud's Bitters Makes a Better Drink.

## RECIPES

### OLD FASHIONED

1½ oz. Blended Whiskey,
Bourbon, or Scotch
1 tsp. Very Fine Granulated Sugar
Splash of Club Soda
2-3 dashes Peychaud's Bitters

Shake Peychaud Bitters, then club soda, on sugar. Muddle. Add two ice cubes. Pour in liquor. Garnish with cherry and orange slice. Stir and serve.

### MANHATTAN

1½ oz. Blended Whiskey
¾ oz. Sweet Vermouth
1-2 dashes Peychaud's Bitters

Stir with ice and strain into cocktail glass. Garnish with a cherry.

### MARTINEZ

Pour 4 oz. Gin over ice cube. Add one or two dashes of dry Vermouth to taste and 3 drops of Peychaud's Bitters. Stir and serve in chilled glass with lemon twist.

### WHISKEY SOUR

1½ oz. Blended Whiskey
1 oz. Lemon Juice
1 Egg White
½ tsp. Very Fine Granulated Sugar

Shake with cracked ice. Strain into cocktail glass. For greater smoothness add a dash of Peychaud's Bitters. Garnish with orange slice and cherry.

Sours can also be made using Bourbon, Scotch, Brandy, Vodka, etc.

## HISTORY

In 1793 wealthy plantation owners were forced to flee the island of San Domingo, salvaging what possessions they could.

Many came to the then Spanish Louisiana city of New Orleans. Among the scanty possessions of one Creole refugee was a recipe for the compounding of a liquid tonic called bitters. His name was Antoine Amedie Peychaud and he had been educated as an apothecary.

A. A. Peychaud's fame in the city of his adoption was founded not so much upon the drugs he dispensed as upon his bitters. These bitters, good for what ailed one irrespective of malady, gave an added zest to the potions of cognac brandy he served friends and others who came into his pharmacy. The fame of this dram of brandy spread rapidly. Consequently the bitters found a ready market in the numerous coffee houses of New Orleans.

In such fashion did Peychaud's original bitters come to be used in other recipes through the decades and is today world famous. The life and zest it gives drinks and food has given it an honored place in famous gourmet recipes the world over.

"Easy on the bitters" becomes a thing of the past when you use Peychaud's; because Peychaud's Bitters have been formulated to be used in the exact amount called for in all drink recipes.
Use Peychaud's Bitters and you serve a perfect drink every time.

A promotional sheet, describing the wonders of Peychaud's Aromatic Cocktail Bitters and its use of a variety of drinks. (From the collection of Jared Brown.)

**C**OCKTAIL, IN THE COMMON parlance, loosely describes any kind of mixed drink, usually containing an alcoholic beverage mixed with a fruit juice or other variety of "mixer," such as tonic or seltzer water. *Webster's New Collegiate Dictionary* defines it as "an iced drink of distilled liquor mixed with flavoring ingredients."[1] There is no clear consensus as to the term's etymological origins, or how the drink itself originated. This paper will focus in detail on the man behind New Orleans' version of the Cocktail's origin: a nineteenth-century pharmacist by the name of Antoine Amedee Peychaud, who has been credited with not only inventing the Cocktail, but also coining the term itself, by virtue of his method of serving a brandy and bitters drink that likely evolved into the classic New Orleans drink, the Sazerac.[2]

## POPULAR THEORIES, ORIGIN OF TERM COCKTAIL

**I**n his seminal work, *The American Language*,[3] H.L. Mencken examines the origins of many words viewed as being of American origin. Many of these terms have to do with "the inspiring vocabulary of bibbing," i.e., relating to the enjoyment of alcoholic beverages. Mencken continues:

> The Cocktail, to multitudes of foreigners, seems to be the greatest symbol of the American way of life, but the etymology

---

1. *Webster's New Collegiate Dictionary* (1979), p. 213.
2. Stanley Clisby Arthur, *Old New Orleans*, Ninth Edition (1950) pp. 37-38.
3. H.L. Mencken, *The American Language—An Inquiry into the Development of English in the United States*, One Volume Abridged Edition (1989), pp. 160-163.

of its name is unknown, and the thing itself may not be of American origin. Of the numerous etymologies the only ones showing any plausibility are the following:

That the word comes from the French *coquetier*, an eggcup, and was first used in New Orleans soon after 1800.[4]

That it is derived from *coquetel*, the name of a mixed drink known in the vicinity of Bordeaux and introduced to America by French officers during the (American) Revolution.

That it descends from cock ale, a mixture of ale and the essence of a boiled fowl, traced by the *Oxford English Dictionary* to c. 1648 in England.

That its parent was a later cock ale, meaning a mixture of spirits and bitters fed to fighting cocks in training.

That it comes from cock-tailed, "having the tail docked so that the short stump sticks up like a cock's tail."

That it is a shortened form of cock tailings, the name of a mixture of tailings from various liquors, thrown together in a common receptacle and sold at a low price.

That "in the days of cock-fighting, the spectators used to toast the cock with the most feathers left in its tail after the contest," and "the number of ingredients in the drink correspond with the number of feathers left."

Mencken concludes this list with the comment, "All are somewhat fishy." He adds, "[a] Cocktail today consists essentially of any hard liquor, any milder diluent and a dash of any pungent flavoring. The *Dictionary of American English's* (DAE's)[5] first example of the word's use—dated

---

4. Here, Mencken inserts a footnote, which reads, "The Cocktail, America's Drink, Was Originated in New Orleans," *Roosevelt Review* (house organ of the Roosevelt Hotel, New Orleans,) April, 1943, pp. 30-1. This unsigned article attributes the Cocktail to Antoine Amedee Peychaud, inventor of Peychaud's Bitters. Since he used brandy made by Sazerac du Forge et Fils, of Limoges, his cocktails were called Sazeracs. Rye whiskey later replaced the brandy.

5. *Dictionary of American English on Historical Principles*, edited by W.A. Craigie and James R. Hulbert; 4 vols.; Chicago, 1938-44.

1806—shows that it was then compounded of "spirits of any kind, sugar, water and bitters," and notes, "this is the basic formula for the Old-Fashioned; hence, perhaps, its name.[6]" Mencken also noted that while many terms in the contemporary lexicon of libations date from antebellum America, they were strangely absent in the dictionaries of that day:

> A majority of terms still used by American boozers —and taken by them from Stockholm to Sydney—date from the gaudy era before the Civil War. Here the DAE and the DA[7] offer less help than they should, for the editors seem to have fought shy of the inspiring vocabulary of bibbing. For example, New Orleans, one of the citadels of Christian drinking during the dry era, has benefited mankind by developing the Sazerac Cocktail and the Gin Fizz; both of these blessings are ignored.[8]

## FIRST KNOWN APPEARANCE OF THE TERM COCKTAIL IN PRINT

As Mencken noted, the *Dictionary of American English*'s "first example of the use of the word" Cocktail was in 1806.[9] This likely refers to the earliest known printed reference, in an editorial appearing on May 6, 1806 in the Hudson, NY newspaper, *The Balance and Columbian Repository*. The editorial blamed a local candidate's recent election defeat on his notori-

---

6. H.L. Mencken, *The American Language—An Inquiry into the Development of English in the United States, One Volume Abridged Edition* (1989), p. 163.

7. *Dictionary of Americanisms on Historical Principles*, edited by Mitford M. Mathews, Chicago, (1951).

8. H.L. Mencken, *The American Language—An Inquiry into the Development of English in the United States, One Volume Abridged Edition* (1989), pp. 160-163.

9. Ibid., pp. 160-161.

ous drinking habit. The editorial prompted a letter to the editor one week later, seeking an explanation of what a Cocktail is:

Sir,

I observe in your paper of the 6th instant, in the account of a democratic candidate for a seat in the Legislature, marked under the head of Loss,'25 do. cock-tail.' Will you be so obliging as to inform me what is meant by this species of refreshment? Though a stranger to you, I believe, from your general character, you will not suppose this request to be impertinent.

I have heard of a jorum, of phlegm-cutter and fog driver, of wetting the whistle, or moistening the clay, of a fillip, a spur in the head, quenching the spark in the head, of slip, etc., but never in my life, though I have lived a good many years, did I hear of cock-tail before. Is it peculiar to this part of the country? Or is it a late invention? Is the name expressive of the effect which the drink has on a particular part of the body? Or does it signify that the democrats who take the potion are turned topsyturvy, and have their heads where their tails should be? I should think the latter to be the real solution; but am unwilling to determine finally until I receive all the information in my power.

At the beginning of the revolution, a physician publically recommended the moss which grew on a tree as a substitute for tea. He found on experiment, that it had more of a stimulating quality than he approved; and therefore, he afterward as publically denounced it. Whatever cock-tail is, it may be properly administered at certain times and to certain constitutions. A few years ago, when the democrats were bawling for Jefferson and Clinton, one of the polls was held in the city of New York at a place where ice cream was sold. Their temperament then was remarkably adust and bilious. Something was necessary to cool them. Now when they are sunk into frigidity, it may be equally necessary, by cock-tail, to warm and rouse them.

I hope you will construe nothing that I have said as disrespectful. I read your paper with great pleasure, and wish it the most extensive circulation. Whether you answer my inquiry or not, I shall remain,

Yours,

A SUBSCRIBER

(the Editor's reply follows)

As I make it a point, never to publish anything (under my editorial head) but what I can explain, I shall not hesitate to gratify the curiosity of my inquisitive correspondent:—Cock tail, then, is a stimulating liquor, composed of spirits of any kind, sugar, water, and bitters—it is vulgarly called bittered sling, and is supposed to be an excellent electioneering potion, inasmuch as it renders the heart stout and bold, at the same time that it fuddles the head. It is said also, to be of great use to a democratic candidate: because, a person having swallowed a glass of it, is ready to swallow anything else.

Edit. Bal.

As an aside, I gratefully acknowledges the survival of the Cocktail over its 1806 contemporaries, noting the romance, sophistication and savoir faire associated with the term. It is difficult to imagine dancing to Glenn Miller's "Moonlight Phlegm-Cutter," I in my blue serge suit, my wife in her black fog-driver dress. But I digress.

Countless others' explanations have been offered as to the origin of the term cocktail. For example, Ted Haigh's book, *Vintage Spirits & Forgotten Cocktails*, presents the following theory:

Cocktails were morning drinks. Nobody knows for sure, but I feel certain they were named Cocktails because they were your wakeup call—like a rooster heralding the early morning light. Now, as much as times change, human nature stays the same. People were largely outraged at the Cocktail much as they remain indignant today about morning drinking. Drinking in the morning often means getting over what you were drinking the night before, and that kind of behavior is what they used to call 'dissipated.'"[10]

To the list of possible birthplaces of the term, add the state of Maryland. Washington Irving's *Knickerbocker's History of New York* discusses the security of Peter Stuyvesant's fledgling Dutch colony:

...his most formidable enemy was the roaring, roistering English colony of Maryland, or, as it was anciently written, Merryland; so called because the inhabitants, not having the fear of the Lord before their eyes, were prone to make merry and get fuddled with Mint-Julep and Apple-Toddy. They were, moreover, great horse-racers and cock-fighters, mighty wrestlers and jumpers, and enormous consumers of hoe-cake and bacon. They lay claim tobe the first inventors of those recondite beverages, Cock-Tail, Stone-Fence, and Sherry-Cobbler, and to have discovered the gastronomical merits of terrapins, soft crabs, and canvas-back ducks.

This rantipole colony, founded by Lord Baltimore, a British nobleman, was managed by his agent, a swaggering Englishman, commonly called Fendall, that is to say, "offend all," a name given him for his bullying propensities. These were seen in a message to Mynheer Beekman, threatening him, unless he immediately swore allegiance to Lord Baltimore as the rightful lord of the soil, to come at the head of the roaring boys of Merryland and the giants of the Susquehanna, and sweep him and his Nederlanders out of the country.[11]

10. Ted Haigh, *Vintage Spirits & Forgotten Cocktails* (2004), p. 10.
11. Washington Irving, *Knickerbocker's History of New York* (1809), p. 241.

# NEW ORLEANS COCKTAIL LORE,
# ANTOINE AMEDEE PEYCHAUD

Unique among these and other theories is the one relating to Antoine Amedee Peychaud, simply because it is centered around an actual person, not some amorphous custom or tradition. This distinction allows us to investigate the theory in more detail, with a greater ability to prove or disprove its elements, and to "carbon date," so to speak, aspects of the theory against other established entities, including historical or cultural context. The impossibility of "proving a negative" appears to be the main stumbling block of many these theories. While this is true with portions of the anecdotal "Cocktail Invented/Coined by Peychaud" theory, certain elements can be examined with some degree of certainty. The following questions surface (with summary answers):

Did Peychaud exist? Yes.

Was he an admixture of fact and folkore in the tradition of Johnny Appleseed, Paul Bunyan and even George Washington? Perhaps.

Was he indeed a pharmacist, born in the Caribbean colony of St.-Domingue, who actually escaped with his life during the slave rebellions? Yes, yes and yes.

Did Peychaud concoct his own brand of aromatic bitters? Yes, and they remain on the market today, known as Peychaud's Aromatic Cocktail Bitters®, made by the Sazerac Company, Inc. of New Orleans.

Did Peychaud bring the recipe for these aromatic bitters with him from St.-Domingue? Unknown, however, if he did, they were likely tucked into his short-pants, as he was a very young child. Or perhaps his nurse brought it with them, who knows?

Did he serve brandy and his own bitters in a *coquetier* (pronounced kah-kuh-TYAY)? Probably, at least, there is no reason to believe that he didn't, and assuming local historians are correct.

Was this offering the prototype of the signature New Orleans Cocktail, the Sazerac? Most likely yes, given the above caveat.

Did Peychaud "invent" the Cocktail, and/or was his method of serving his brandy, sugar and bitters concoction the origin of the term? Perhaps locally, however not globally.

Did Antoine Amedee Peychaud have a career in politics prior to becoming a pharmacist? No. While he was a member of the Whig party,[12] he did not hold office or run for mayor in 1828. However, his cousin Anatole Peychaud did (*see below*).

## ORIGINS OF A LEGEND

As noted above, local legend maintains that the Cocktail was born in New Orleans, both the name and the drink itself. As the story goes, the term "Cocktail" arose out of the manner in which a brandy-based concoction was served to customers by nineteenth-century New Orleans pharmacist, Antoine Amedee Peychaud.[13]

New Orleans was settled by the French in 1718, and for the first 100-plus years was populated primarily by persons of French descent. The Louisiana Purchase occurred in 1803, and Louisiana became a state in 1812.[14] As more and more English-speaking Americans migrated to New

---

12. *New Orleans Bee*, July 1, 1843.
13. Stanley Clisby Arthur, *Old New Orleans, Ninth Edition* (1950), pp. 37-38.
14. *Encyclopaedia Britannica*, Vol. 30 (1984), pp. 6-7.

Orleans, so the story goes, the pronunciation subsequently suffered, and *coquetier* blurred, or rather slurred, into Cocktail. This story can be found in published accounts dating back to the 1930s and 1940s including, as noted above, Mencken's *The American Language*.[15] In his 1936 book, *Old New Orleans*, historian Stanley Clisby Arthur offers an explanation of not only the origins of the term "Cocktail," but of its invention itself:

> ...the Cocktail is born—437 Royal Street—This antique shop
> ... holds an interest not usually the run of old furniture and
> trinket places ... for here was conceived and born that pecu-
> liar and throat-satisfying liquid concoction—the American
> Cocktail. Here, too, so a well-authenticated tradition
> informs us, was this popular drink given its name.

The notarial acts consulted inform us that this building, and its corner twin, was erected in 1800 by Don Jose Pavis, and that, in 1816 Nicholas Girod, the Mayor of New Orleans, purchased the property for $32,000. Be that as it may, our interest lies in its first tenant—a native of San Domingo, forced to flee that island by the uprising of the blacks in 1795, who here opened a successful and popular drug store. The apothecary's name was Antoine Amedee Peychaud, one of the Dominguois who flocked to Spanish Louisiana when the blacks drove them from their island in the sunlit Caribbean.

New Orleans owes much to these French-speaking islanders. To them are due the first newspaper in Louisiana, the first theatre and the cultivation of sugar cane. To these white Dominguois is also due the word "Creole," which we use to distinguish the native Louisianian of

---

15. The story apparently first appeared in *Arthur's Old New Orleans* in 1936, then in his 1937 book *Famous New Orleans Drinks and How to Mix 'Em*, then in the January, 1938 magazine *Roosevelt Review*, in the 1938 *New Orleans City Guide*, published by the Federal Writers Project, then again in the *Roosevelt Review* in April, 1943.

French or Spanish descent. The word was Spanish, and first applied only to the descendants of Spanish colonists born in the New World, but the use of the term spread to the French West Indies, and was brought to New Orleans by the refugees from San Domingo. To the above roster of boons given Louisiana by the Dominguois we now must add the word "Cocktail."

A.A. Peychaud's bid for fame and popularity was not founded so much upon the quality of the drugs he dispensed over the counter of his apothecary shop, but in the bitters he compounded and concocted from a secret formulae he reputedly brought with him from his native island. These bitters—good for what ailed you irrespective of the malady—gave an added zest to the potions of cognac brandy he served his cronies in the pharmacy after meetings of his Masonic Lodge, as Peychaud was W.M. of Concorde Blue Lodge, Grand Orator of the Grand Lodge, High Priest of the Royal Arch, and belonged to other divisions of that fraternity, for clearly he was a "joiner." The fame of his highly flavored dram of brandy served by Pharmacie Peychaud spread and the place became a popular rendezvous.

Peychaud had a popular way of serving his concoction. Each potion was mixed in what we now call the double-ended egg cup. The French-speaking folk of Old New Orleans knew this piece of table crockery as a *coquetier*, and those who could not properly pronounce French called the libation a "cock-tay," or, possibly, through sampling too many of Peychaud's spiced brandies, the English-speaking were soon designating them as "Cocktails."[16]

While politically incorrect at times, this is nonetheless a very interesting story. This explanation is also found in another of Arthur's books, *Famous New Orleans Drinks*

---

16. Stanley Clisby Arthur, *Old New Orleans, Ninth Edition* (1950), pp. 37-38.

*and How to Mix 'Em.* In this book, Arthur further concludes that Peychaud's *coquetier* "was, in all probability, fore-
runner of the present jigger—the name given the double-
end metal contraption holding a jigger (1.5 ounces) in the
big end, and a pony (1 ounce) in the little end, which we
now use to measure portion for mixed drinks.[17]" He further
writes:

> The Birth of the Cocktail—In the year 1793, at the time of
> the uprising of the blacks on the portion of the island of San
> Domingo then belonging to France, wealthy white planta-
> tion owners were forced to flee that favored spot in the sun-
> lit Caribbean. With them went their precious belongings and
> heirlooms. Some of the expelled Domenguais who flocked
> to what was then Spanish Louisiana brought gold to Louisiana.
> Others brought slaves along with their household goods. Some
> brought nothing but the clothes they wore upon their backs.
> One refugee succeeded in salvaging, among other scanty pos-
> sessions, a recipe for the compounding of a liquid tonic, called
> bitters, a recipe that had been a family secret for years.

This particular young Creole refugee—Antoine
Amedee Peychaurd—was of a distinguished French
family and had been educated as an apothecary.
Arthur continues:

> The fame of Peychaud's highly flavored dram of brandy spread
> rapidly. Consequently the bitters found a ready market in the
> numerous coffee houses (as liquid dispensing establishments
> were then called) that stood cheek by jowl in almost every
> street in old New Orleans. Cognac had long been a popu-
> lar drink among the city's experienced bibbers, but presently
> customers began demanding their French brandy spiked with
> a dash or so of the marvelous bitters compounded by M.
> Peychaud.[18]

---

17. Stanley Clisby Arthur, *Famous New Orleans Drinks And How to Mix 'Em* (1937, 1989), pp. 9-11.
18. Ibid., p. 11.

Arthur's treatise on Peychaud's Cocktail is careful to distinguish the ordinary Brandy Toddy from the distinctive Brandy Cocktail. He also discusses the many imitators that sprang up to ride the Peychaud Cocktail's coattails, but points out that "Peychaud's original San Domingo bitters gave an otherwise simple brandy toddy new life and zest. In such fashion did the inconspicuous little crockery *coquetier* become the christening font of the Cocktail!"[19]

## PEYCHAUD FAMILY ORIGINS IN BORDEAUX AND THE CARIBBEAN

The Peychaud family originally hailed from the Bordeaux region of western France, specifically in the neighboring villages of Bourg-sur-Gironde and Blaye.[20] For centuries, the Peychaud family was renown in the winemaking business; translated, Peychaud means "of the warm hill," likely referring to terrain favorable to growing grapes. To this day, there are two wineries, Chateau Peychaud and Chateau Peychaud Maisonneuve, offering fine Bordeaux wines. Through the centuries, many Peychauds have served as Mayor of Bourg, and also as First Jurat, an elected position, similar to City Council Chairman. So in France, the Peychauds were wealthy landowners and prominent members of society.[21]

It was some time during the last half of the eighteenth century that two branches of the Peychaud family—one led by Hyacinthe Mathias Peychaud, the other by his cousin Charles Peychaud—left France to seek their fortune in the

---

19. Stanley Clisby Arthur, *Famous New Orleans Drinks And How to Mix 'Em* (1937, 1989), p. 11.
20. Charles Amedee Maurian, *Famille Peychaud* (1908), pp. 1-3.
21. Ibid., pp. 1-2.

New World, and settled in St.-Domingue. Both became wealthy and established planters, and lived there until forced to leave during the slave rebellions of the 1790s through 1800s.[22]

Charles Peychaud owned a coffee plantation,[23] and was deeply involved in politics.[24] His son, Dr. Charles Louis Peychaud, was a physician. This Peychaud and his wife Rosalie Martinet had a daughter, Lasthenie (around 1799) and then a son, Antoine Amedee Peychaud.[25]

It is believed that Antoine was born on February 24, 1803 in the port city of Cap-Français (now Cap-Haitien), on the colony's northern coast.[26] Beginning in August of 1791, following a voodoo ceremony, the slaves of St.-Domingue began a rebellion that lasted over twelve years, resulting in the overthrow of the French colonial government, the death or expulsion of most of the white, French landowners, and the birth of the nation of Haiti.[27]

## ANTOINE AMEDEE PEYCHAUD'S PERILOUS EXODUS FROM ST.-DOMINGUE

ccording to several published accounts, Antoine Amedee Peychaud was a small child when the rebellions ultimately reached his

22. Stanley Clisby Arthur, *Famous New Orleans Drinks And How to Mix 'Em* (1937, 1989), pp. 1-4.

23. *Indemnity Lists, Commission Chargie de Reportir L'Indemnitite Atribuee Ais Anciens Colons de St.-Domingue*, Ministry de Finances, Frances, Library of Congress, Call No. HJ 8951 F8A3.

24. Ph. Wright and Gabriel Debien, *Les Colons de Saint-Domingue Passes a la Jamaique (1792-1835)*, Notes D'Histoire Coloniale—No. 168, Extrait du Bulletin de la Societe d'Histoire de la Guadeloupe, No. 26, 4th Trimestre (1975), pp. 49-50.

25. Correspondence with Michel Peychaud, Bordeaux, France.

26. Ibid. Further, Peychaud's year of birth is corroborated by two newspaper death notices, noted below.

27. Footnote to *Encyclopedia Americana, International Edition* (1998), pp. 701-702.

grandparents' coffee plantation in the village of Margot, near the northern coastal town of Le Borgne, just west of Cap-Français.[28] During the confusion and chaos, he was separated from his family as a hurried evacuation took place. He ultimately ended up in New Orleans, as did thousands of other French colonists fleeing the rebellions. Many such refugees lived for a time in Cuba, and some in Jamaica, before ultimately coming to New Orleans. However it is not known when Peychaud came to New Orleans, with whom, and whether or not he lived in Cuba, Jamaica or elsewhere.[29] It is known that another branch, led by his cousin Hyacinthe Mathias Peychaud, lived several years in Kingston, Jamaica before coming to New Orleans, probably in 1803. Perhaps he lived with them and/or they helped raise him upon his arrival in New Orleans.[30]

More details of Peychaud's perilous escape can be found in the 1921 book, *Creole Families of New Orleans*, by renowned New Orleans historian Grace King:

> Peychaud and his sister Lasthenie were saved from massacre in the insurrection of the slaves by their nurse, but in the panic of the moment the children became separated and the boy was brought to New Orleans. As he grew to manhood he never ceased to long for his sister and to search for her. At last he heard that she was living in Paris; he sent for her and had her brought to New Orleans. As the ship came up the river Peychaud stood on the levee waiting for her. She was the first passenger to step on the plank and walk to the shore. As she did so, a gust of wind blew aside her skirt and revealed the most beautiful foot and ankle in the world— at least so thought a young man standing in the crowd to watch the ship arrive. He sought her acquaintance (gentle-

---

28. Footnote to *Creole Families of New Orleans* by Grace King (1921) pp. 332-333; Stanley Clisby Arthur, *Old Families of Louisiana* (1931) pp. 327-328.

29. Louis Moreau Lislet and Rene R. Nicau, "The French Colonists From St. Domingue and, in Particular," reprinted in *New Orleans Genesis*, Vol. XXIX, No. 113 (January, 1990), pp. 3-4.

30. Grace King, *Creole Families of New Orleans* (1921), pp. 331.

men at that time acted on such impulses), found her face as beautiful as her foot, and then he sought her in marriage (as a gentleman of that time would do), and he did not seek in vain. Lasthenie became his wife and he, in time, became a distinguished judge.[31]

This "distinguished judge" was Charles Auguste de Besse de Maurian (1786–1858).[32] Lasthenie Peychaud and Judge Maurian had but one child, Charles Amedee Maurian, during whose childbirth Lasthenie tragically died.[33] Charles Amedee Maurian, Antione's nephew, went on to become an accomplished chess player, and was a close friend and favorite chess partner of the great world chess champion and fellow Orleanian, Paul Morphy.[34]

It is important to note that Grace King's 1921 account of Antoine Amedee Peychaud's childhood exodus from St.-Domingue was corroborated by Charles Amedee Maurian's 1912 obituary,[35] thus lending some degree of credibility to Grace King's story. It is significant if only to dispel the notion that Peychaud was an adult when he came to New Orleans from St.-Domingue, or that he was already a pharmacist.

## PEYCHAUD
## THE NEW ORLEANS PHARMACIST

The earliest known reference to A.A. Peychaud as an adult in New Orleans is found in local newspapers from the year 1832, when a notice was published by one A. Duconge to announce his new

31. Grace King, *Creole Families of New Orleans* (1921), pp. 332-333.
32. Ronald R. Morazan, *Biographical Sketches of the Veterans of the Battalion of New Orleans, 1814-1815* (1979), p. 155.
33. Grace King,*Creole Families of New Orleans* (1921) p. 333.
34. David Lawson, *Paul Morphy: the Pride and Sorrow of Chess* (1976).
35. Copy available but date and newspaper unknown.

pharmacy partnership with Peychaud. This ad appeared in the *New Orleans Bee* of July 5, 1832:

> The undersigned, having taken Mr. Antony (shown as "Antoine" in the French version) Peychaud in partnership, will continue his business from this date under the firm of Duconge & Peychaud.

In addition to pharmaceutical and medicinal goods, Duconge & Peychaud also sold botanical and agricultural items, such as trees, greenhouse shrubs, herbaceous plants, roots and seeds from their address at 89 Chartres Street.[36] Perhaps it was this exposure to herbs, roots and botanicals that aided young Peychaud in the compounding of his famous bitters.

By March of 1834, the partnership of Duconge and Peychaud had dissolved, and at age 31, Peychaud opened his own pharmacy.[37] (Duconge continued to operate his pharmacy for many years on his own. The 1838 City Directory lists Duconge as a druggist, residing at 41 Orleans Street, and his ads could be seen into the 1860s in local media.[38]) To announce his new venture, Peychaud ran a front page ad in the *New Orleans Bee* of March 20, 1834:

> THE undersigned informs his friends and the public at large, that he has purchased the Drug and Apothecary Store, lately belonging to Mr. Prats, No. 123 Royal Street, between St. Louis and Conti Streets. He will have constantly on hand, a complete assortment of Drugs, Medicines, Chymical Preparations, Surgical Instruments, &c., the whole of the best quality, and on accommodating terms; the orders of the country will be punctually and faithfully attended to, as will the prescriptions of professional gentlemen. He hopes that the man-

---

36. *New Orleans Bee*, January 3, 1833.
37. *New Orleans Bee*, March 20, 1834.
38. *New Orleans Bee*, January 2, 1860, *New Orleans Bee*, February 2, 1860, et al.

ner of performing the duties of his profession, will secure him the confidence of all those who will apply to him.

In 1834, Peychaud was not only concerned with the launching of his new pharmacy, he was active in a popular movement to eliminate, or at least control, the widespread and increasingly lethal practice of dueling in New Orleans. The following is an excerpt from *New Orleans, The Glamour Period, 1800-1840* by Albert E. Fossier. Chapter XXXV is called "Measuring Swords and Exchanging Shots," and concerns the city's dueling epidemic:

> In the 1830s the number of duels rose to formidable proportions and many steps were taken to suppress the abuse. According to the Bee of September 3, 1834, a meeting was called for the purpose of decreasing the number of duels and to establish a court of honor. Bernard Marigny and General Plauche were its presidents, assisted by Donatien Augustin, Douce and Mercier. The meeting took place at Davis Hall on Monday, September 16. It was very well attended....[40]

Among the list of names of subscribers, which included New Orleans mayor Denis Prieur and many other New Orleans luminaries, was none other than A.A. Peychaud. Thus, to the list of what we know about Antoine

---

39. The system of New Orleans street numbering has undergone several changes over the years, and I have been advised by researchers at the Historic New Orleans Collection that 123 Royal Street, circa 1834, is now 437 Royal, which now houses James H. Cohen and Sons, a rare coin and antique gun dealer. The 1838 New Orleans City Directory lists Peychaud as a "druggist, 123 Royal," and this is the first of many annual references to him in this capacity (the 1842 City Directory identifies him as "druggist and chemist." The City Directories from 1849 to 1861 list him as "druggist, 108 Royal." It may well be that this the same physical location as the "123 Royal" address, due to the changing of street numberings that often took place. However, the 1861 City Directory, published on the eve of the Civil War, showed him at both the 108 Royal location and at 90 Royal, so perhaps he had expanded to two locations. The 1842 City Directory, which is cross-referenced by address, shows that A.A. had two employees; A. Donnaud was "assistant druggist," and a Dr. Doussan also was in an employee "at A.A. Peychaud."

40. Albert E. Fossier, *New Orleans, The Glamour Period, 1800-1840*, p. 443.

Amedee Peychaud, he was concerned about the proliferation of dueling. Pistols for two, Cocktail for one, indeed.

## PEYCHAUD
## AND HIS AROMATIC BITTERS

As we know, Peychaud concocted and marketed his own brands of aromatic bitters. According to mixologist Dale DeGroff, "Peychaud him-self made his bitters on a small scale but in 1840 the prod-uct was manufactured and sold nationally and interna-tionally."[41] As these bitters grew in popularity, they also garnered much recognition. They received the Diploma of Honor at the Grand Exhibition of Altona, Germany in 1869, and won medals at events in New Orleans (Gold Medal, 1884-85), Atlanta (Bronze Medal, 1895), St. Louis (Gold Medal, 1904), Portland (Gold Medal, 1905) and Jamestown, NY (Highest Award, 1907).[42]

Peychaud aggressively marketed his bitters, competing against such established national brands as Baker's and Hostetter's. On June 27, 1857, and throughout that month, Amedee ran an ad on the front page of the *New Orleans Bee*:

AMERICAN AROMATIC BITTER CORDIAL

This cordial, whose delicate flavor and aroma are unsurpassed, is the most successful restorative and tonic known in cases of general debility; it restores the appetite, invigorates the action and functions of the stomach, and thereby prevents dyspepsia, so often brought on by continued attacks of indi-gestion, the prevalent of hot and humid climates. Said cor-dial may be administered with equal efficacy to the infant

41. Dale De Groff, *The Craft of the Cocktail*, (2002), p. 6.
42. Peychaud's Aromatic Cocktail Bitters® label.

and the aged, by following the directions printed on the label *And Other Things* of each bottle, and its agreeable taste is not the least of its recommendations.

This cordial has been introduced into general use in the Sazerac House, and other principal Coffee-Houses in this city, as far superior to Baker's Stomach Bitters, so celebrated throughout the United States, and there can be no doubt that all who have tasted the AMERICAN CORDIAL, give it the preference over all other bitters in use.

This advertisement is significant in that it mentions the Sazerac House, which "places the suspect at the scene," so to speak. In other words, it helps to corroborate the belief that Peychaud's Bitters were used in mixing the original —brandy-based—Sazerac, and were an essential part of that famous New Orleans drink.

On April 19, 1858, and throughout the month, Amedee ran a front page ad in the *New Orleans Bee*:

TONI-AROMATIC BITTERS

A Cordial for Ladies and Aged Persons

THIS highly agreeable cordial is taken pure, and was prepared by me at the request of a number of families who had represented to me the inconvenience resulting from using those varieties of bitters which cannot be imbibed undiluted, the loss of time which they occasion, and the mistakes made from ignorance of the mode of administering them.

These well founded objections enabled me to understand the true causes which deter many persons from making use of their excellent and beneficial preparations. The one manufactured by me, to be taken pure, obviates all the difficulties alluded to. It is highly efficacious in cases of general weakness, and in nervous affections generally, and is a preventative from gastritis—that fatal disease so peculiar in warm and humid climates. It re-establishes the appetite, invigorates the general system, and in time restores a healthy color in persons who have acquired a lymphatic temperament.

This cordial possesses not only the property of stimulating the appetite, but of aiding digestion. If tempted by a sumptious repast to indulge beyond the bounds of prudence, we suffer from a slow and impeded digestion, a small drop of the admirable liquor occasions speedy relief and facilitates the work of nature.

Persons in good health may use it as a preservative and pleasant beverage. Its delicious aroma and taste render it such. Those who are in the habit of taking lunch, and particularly ladies, will find it an invaluable addition in this repast, not merely on account of its exquisite flavor, but from the digestive qualities.

The most delicate constitutions, from infancy to old age, of both sexes, may employ it without the slightest inconvenience.

Directions will be given to persons using it for the first time.

Less than a year later, on March 1, 1859, Peychaud ran no fewer than three front page ads in the *New Orleans Bee*. These ads refer to two varieties of bitters offered by Peychaud. One of the ads concerned Peychaud's "American Aromatic Bitters," the other again referred to his "Toni-Aromatic Bitters." The third ad was disguised as a letter to the editor, and nowadays would likely be one of those advertisements that is presented to the eye as a news article, however with the words "advertisement" at the top:

[communicated]

Useful to the Human Race

To the Editors of the Bee:

When the Bitters prepared by Mr. A.A. Peychaud become thoroughly known, when everyone understands the value of his Toni-Aromatic, and his American Aromatic Bitters— the first to be taken pure, and the second diluted—there will be few families willing to do without them. By mixing the strongest in such quantity as may be desired with a small cordial glassfull of the weakest, a beverage is obtained which can be rendered more or less powerful to suit the taste. As for ladies, aged persons and children, the Toni-Aromatic Bitters, which are taken pure, will best agree with them. Nevertheless a small quantity of the stronger article may be added to please the taste of those who desire it.

So delightful and precious a compound—one so essential to the preservation of health—might be taken as habitually as food and drink, with the perfect certainty that its use will prolong life and invigorate health.

This "testimonial" appeared in column six of the front page. In column five Peychaud ran a second ad, which read as follows:

American Aromatic Bitters

It is with unfeigned pleasure we bear our testimony to the efficacy of these Bitters. There have been so many spurious articles offered to the public that we were determined to test the qualifications of them all, and we give a decided preference to the kind now heading this article. It is without a competitor, and one of the best proofs of this is that you cannot go into any public place without finding it. We use it in our own house, and its revivifying principle is astonishing. If you have any biliary or liver complaint; if you should be recovering from fever of any description; if you are weak or very debilitated; in fact, If you have any weak point at all about your system, then we say, take the American aromatic bitters.

It is a powerful restorative, and can be taken with wine, spirits or any kind of beverage.

The third ad appeared in column nine of the March 1, 1859 *New Orleans Bee*:

Toni-Aromatic Bitters

A DELICIOUS CORDIAL FOR LADIES AND OLD PEOPLE, &c., &c.

THESE TONI-AROMATIC BITTERS, possessing the most delightful perfume and flavor, are prepared to be taken pure, even by the most delicate persons. This preparation has the valuable property of invigorating and re-establishing the animal economy in all cases of general debility. Its habitual use dissipates nervous affections, fortifies the stomach, stimulates the appetite, and permanently strengthens and improves digestion. This special quality enables it to prevent and counteract diseases of the liver, and those gastric affectations which are so frequently produced by an impaired digestion. Prepared and sold by

A.A. PEYCHAUD

Bitters, and other forms of patent medicine, were extremely popular in America during the 1850s, and the March 1, 1859 issue of the *Bee* evidences this. By publishing three ads on the front page, Peychaud was endeavoring to compete with a strong national brand, Hostetter's Stomach Bitters, which itself had two ads (one of which occupied several column-inches of type). Indeed, within this one issue of the *Bee* there are over a dozen advertisements for bitters and patent medicine, including such other offerings as:

- Dr. J. Hostetter's Celebrated Stomach Bitters
- Dr. Brunan's Bitters
- Boerhave's Holland Bitters
- Richardson's Sherry Wine Bitters
- Dr. McLane's Celebrated Vermifuge
  (for treating tapeworm)
- Dr. McLane's Celebrated Liver Pills

- Holloways Pills and Ointment (for dyspepsia)
- Dr. Ham's Aromatic Invigorating Spirit
- Dr. Q.J. Leeds Quinine Substitute
- Peruvian Syrup
- P. Gaudin's Invigorating and Nutritive Pomatum
- Ayer's Cherry Pectoral, Cathartic Pills and Ague Cure
- Hippolyte Brieugne's Anti-Gouty Elixir, and
- Benriquez' Antephelic Milk

It should also be noted that in addition to Peychaud's Bitters, Lea & Perrins' Celebrated Worcestershire Sauce was also among the products advertised in that edition that have survived to this day. Perhaps it is not a coincidence that both products are essential to classic Cocktails, the Sazerac and the Bloody Mary.

## LATER MANUFACTURE OF PEYCHAUD'S BITTERS, COMPETITION

**S**uffice it to say, competition was fierce in the bitters market in the latter half of the nineteenth century. Peychaud's Bitters became a very successful brand and has endured to this day as among the leading domestic sellers, with a growing overseas market share, according to its current maker, Sazerac Company, Inc. At some point along the line, however, Peychaud fell upon tough financial times. In 1869, he was forced to sell his pharmacy property at 90 Royal Street, as well as stock holdings in the Citizen's Bank of Louisiana, valued at $13,075.[43] In 1876, Peychaud was a clerk at the pharmacy of H.J. Rivet, at 58 Chartres Street.[44] Peychaud sold his interests—formula and brand name—in his aromatic bitters to a former employee, Thomas Handy, and became an employee of Thomas H. Handy & Company.[45]

Handy continued to make and market Peychaud's Bitters, however, in 1880, some three years prior to Peychaud's death, Handy decided to change the name from Peychaud's Bitters to Handy's Bitters, and simply inserted the name Handy on the label where Peychaud had been. This was done with Peychaud's conscious acquiescence. Another former employee of Peychaud, Anthony Commander, also decided to go into the bitters business. In designing his label, Commander mimicked Handy (who had earlier mimicked Peychaud) by inserting the name "Commander's" in the same place where the name "Peychaud's" and "Handy's" had earlier appeared on the label. What resulted was a nearly identical label. Handy sued Commander for trademark infringement and won.[46]

Interestingly, Anthony Commander was reportedly of the same family that founded the famous New Orleans restaurant, Commander's Palace. The 1888 City Directory shows Commander to be a bartender at the Sazerac Saloon, and in 1889 he opened his own restaurant, Bon-Ton Café, at No. 36 Magazine Street.[47]

## THE PEYCHAUD HOUSE

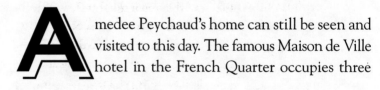

A medee Peychaud's home can still be seen and visited to this day. The famous Maison de Ville hotel in the French Quarter occupies three

---

43. Orleans Parish Notary Archive, Conveyance Office, Book 94, p. 458.

44. 1876 New Orleans City Directory

45. Thomas Handy & Co. v. A. Commander, Supreme Court of Louisiana, Archived Trial Proceedings, Louisiana Supreme Court Archive, p. 23.

46. Thomas Handy & Co. v. A. Commander, 49 La.Ann. 1119, 22 So. 230 (1897), p. 1121.

47. New Orleans Public Library's Web site, online exhibit, "*Que La Fete Commence!*" at http://nutrias.org/~nopl/exhibits/french/french2.htm.

buildings, the oldest of which, at 727 Toulouse Street, also goes by the name "The Peychaud House," as it served as Amedee's home for many years in the first half of the nineteenth century. According to an article in the New Orleans *Times-Picayune*, the hotel (all three buildings) was sold to a group of investors in 1983 for $2.7 million. The article goes on to say that "(i)n room 9 of this building, Tennessee Williams is believed to have completed the final draft of *A Streetcar Named Desire* in the 1940s." The courtyard abuts an adjoining courtyard, the even more famous Court of Two Sisters.[48] From the Hotel Maison de Ville Web site is the following:

> The Maison de Ville, which in French means town house, is just that a two-storied dwelling built by Jean Baptiste Lilie Sarpy, circa 1800. The house was built just after the disastrous fire of 1786. An early resident of the home was Antoine Amedee Peychaud, an apothecary who developed a concoction of bitters and brandy, measured in a *coquetier* or egg cup. Peychaud is often credited as developing the first Cocktail. Peychaud Bitters, still produced today, are used in a traditional New Orleans Cocktail called Sazerac. Although in many Creole homes of the time the first floor was used as a store or office, we know that Peychaud maintained his pharmacy on nearby Royal Street.
>
> Before he purchased his own house in the French Quarter, Tennessee Williams often stayed in room number 9, where he completed *A Streetcar Named Desire* and drank Sazeracs in the hotel courtyard. The room, which opens onto the patio, was the setting for Dick Cavett's 1974 interview with Williams — surrounding him by the lush semi-tropical greenery and flowers the playwright enjoyed.
>
> Guests to New Orleans can not only attend the annual Tennessee Williams/New Orleans Literary Festival, but also stay

---

48. *New Orleans Times-Picayune*, February 19, 1983

in the same room Mr. Williams wrote one of his most famous works.[49]

## PEYCHAUD'S DEATH

Antoine Amedee Peychaud died at the age of 80 on June 30, 1883, according to death notices published in both the *New Orleans Bee* and the *Daily Picayune* on July 1, 1883. The notice in the *Daily Picayune* notes that Peychaud was living at 8 Laharpe Street—a street that parallels Esplanade/Bayou Road, about 10 blocks north and east of the French Quarter. No cause of death was listed in either notice.

## CONCLUDING DISCUSSION

Having thus examined the factual history as well as the folk legend surrounding Antoine Amedee Peychaud, one can conclude that he did indeed exist, and was a pharmacist and the creator of Peychaud's Aromatic Cocktail Bitters. Further, the story of his perilous exodus from the slave rebellions of St.-Domingue is substantiated both by historians (Grace King, Stanley Clisby Arthur) and newspaper (obituary of his nephew Charles Amedee Maurian, whose 1912 death pre-dated the copyright dates of the works of Arthur and King). It is also very likely that his bitters, sugar and brandy con-coction was the original Sazerac. But what can we con-clude about the legend that insists that Peychaud invented the Cocktail, both as a beverage and as a term?

Given the fact that a very detailed definition of the term Cocktail appeared in a New York newspaper in 1806,

---

49. See www.maisondeville.com/about/history.html.

and the fact that Peychaud's death notice (in two news-papers) listed his age as 80 at the time of his death in June of 1883, one can only conclude that Peychaud did not invent the Cocktail nor did he coin the term, at least on a global basis. It is possible, of course, that Peychaud's man-ner of serving his concoctions in a *coquetier* gave rise to the term in New Orleans. Indeed, during the nineteenth century, New Orleans was known for getting the news late. For example, the Battle of New Orleans was fought more than two weeks after the War of 1812 was concluded by the Treaty of Ghent.[50] News of President Abraham Lin-coln's assassination, which took place on April 14, 1865, did not arrive for nearly a week, and did not appear in the *New Orleans Bee* until April 20. Perhaps use of the term outside of Louisiana had not yet made it to New Orleans from Hudson, NY, and Peychaud's habit of serving drinks in a *coquetier* was in fact the local origination of that term. Like all of the other Cocktail theories, it is a matter of speculation.

Were Peychaud's Bitters prominently used and a house-hold name in nineteenth-century New Orleans? Yes. In fact, Peychaud's Bitters were widely copied, both in sub-stance and in labeling (*see the Handy case, above*).

Were Peychaud's Bitters used in ninetenth-century New Orleans Cocktails? Yes. We know from Peychaud's 1857 newspaper advertisement that his bitters were in "general use in the Sazerac House, and other principal Coffee-Houses in this city,"[51] and can therefore conclude with some certainty that his bitters were a vital component in the original Sazerac and other classic New Orleans drinks. Indeed, in the 1885 *Creole Cook Book—La Cuisine Creole*, Lafcadio Hearn offered the following:

---

50. *Encyclopaedia Britannica*, Vol. 30 (1984), pp. 6-8.
51. *New Orleans Bee*, June 27, 1857.

Whiskey, Brandy or Gin Cocktails—New Orleans Style: Two
dashes of Boker's, Angostura or Peychaud bitters—either will
make a fine cocktail. One lump of sugar, one piece of lemon
peel, one tablespoonful of water, one wine-glassful of liquor,
etc., with plenty of ice. Stir well and strain into a Cocktail
glass.[52]

It is very likely that Brandy Cocktails were popular in
New Orleans in the mid-1830s, whether or not they were
"invented" by Peychaud in any form. In the 1845 book
*New Orleans As I Found It,*[71] Henry Didimus told of his
trip to New Orleans in the winter of 1835-1836, and especially of his first encounter with the Brandy Cocktail. He
was being regaled with the story of a former city employee
who had "resigned his commission" in order to "open up
a dancing house in what was then called 'the Swamp…,'"
and at this dancing-house they proudly served "Brandy-
Cocktails."[72] "The Swamp" was a notorious section of old
New Orleans, in the part of town where the Louisiana
Superdome now resides. Excellent discussions of The
Swamp may be found in *The French Quarter—An Informal History of the New Orleans Underworld,*[55] and *Frenchmen, Desire, Good Children, and Other Streets of New
Orleans.*[56]

Henry Didimus' discussion of the Brandy Cocktail
included the following:

[Indent] "Now the difference between a Brandy-Cocktail and
a Brandy-Toddy is this: A Brandy-Toddy is made by adding
together a little water, a little sugar, and a great deal of
brandy—mix well and drink. A Brandy-Cocktail is composed
of the same ingredients, with the addition of a shade of

---

52. Lafcadio Hearn, *Creole Cook Book—La Cuisine Creole* (1885, republished
1990, Pelican Publishing Company), p. 248.
53. Henry Didimus, *New Orleans As I Found It* (New York: Harper & Bros.,
1845), p. 25.
54. Ibid.

Stoughton's bitters; so that the bitters draw the line of demarcation. Boy, bring up four brandy-toddies—you shall taste the distinction, sir!"

It is interesting to note that Didimus' host referred to Stoughton's Bitters, not Peychaud's. Perhaps Peychaud had not yet concocted and/or commercialized his own bitters; after all, Didimus' trip to New Orleans occurred in 1835-1836, Peychaud's pharmacy opened in March, 1834. Perhaps Peychaud's Bitters were initially served only on-site, at his pharmacy at 123 Royal Street. At venues such as the one Didimus' host frequently visited. they were in the habit of using Stoughton's. In any event, Peychaud's Bitters is the brand that has survived (and thrived) to this day, not Stoughton's.

Are Peychaud's Bitters important to mixologists, both historically and today? Yes. Peychaud's Aromatic Cocktail Bitters were a vital part of New Orleans' original Cocktails,[57] and are today considered indispensable to bartenders around the world, not only as essential in making the proper Sazerac, as well as other drinks.

Did Peychaud invent the Sazerac, or at least its prototype? Possibly, if not probably, if historian Stanley Clisby Arthur can be relied upon, since much of what has heretofore been written about Peychaud (that he dispensed brandy, sugar and bitters from his pharmacy), comes from Arthur. Indeed, he tells us that the original Sazerac contained as its base the same brandy, sugar and bitters concoction that Peychaud first dispensed from his apothecary. Either before or after the addition of absinthe, it became the Sazerac, and became famous from its home just a few

---

55. Herbert Asbury, *The French Quarter – An Informal History of the New Orleans Underworld* (Garden City, NY: Garden City Publishing, 1936).

56. John Chase, *Frenchmen, Desire, Good Children, and Other Streets of New Orleans* (Robert Crager & Company, 1949).

57. "Precious Stone Period of New Orleans Saloons Recalled," *The New Orleans Sunday Item-Tribune*, January 9, 1938, p. 5.

blocks up Royal Street. This is what Arthur has to say about the Sazerac Cocktail's origin in his 1937 book *Famous New Orleans Drinks and How to Mix 'Em*:

> Oldtimers will tell you the three outstanding drinks of New Orleans in the memory of living men were the dripped Absinthe Frappe of the Old Absinthe House, the Ramos Gin Fizz, and the Sazerac Cocktail.
>
> As previously related, the American Cocktail was not only born in New Orleans but was given its curious name in the city's famous Vieux Carre. There are Cocktails and Cocktails, but the best known of all New Orleans Cocktails is unquestionably the Sazerac. The fact that it originated here gave rise to the legend that it was first concocted and named for an old Louisiana family, legend without fact as no such Louisiana family ever existed.
>
> A barbershop now holds forth in a building on the right hand side of the first block in Royal Street going down from Canal, and before its doors, there still remains lettered in the sidewalk the word "SAZERAC." This denotation indicated the entrance-way to a once well-patronized bar on the Exchange Alley side of the building. It was here the drink famed far and wide as the Sazerac Cocktail was mixed and dispensed. It was here it was christened with the name it now bears.

For years one of the favorite brands of cognac imported was the brandy manufactured by Messrs. Sazerac-de-Forge et fils, of Limoges, France. The local agent for this firm was John B. Schiller. In 1859 Schiller opened a liquid dispensary at 13 Exchange Alley, naming it "Sazerac Coffee House" after the brand of cognac served exclusively at his bar.

Schiller's Brandy Cocktails became the drink of the moment and his business flourished, surviving even the War Between the States. In 1870 Thomas H. Handy, his bookkeeper, succeeded as proprietor and changed the name to "Sazerac House." An alteration in the mixture also took place. Peychaud's bitters was still used to add the right fillip, but American rye whiskey was substituted for the French cognac to please the tastes of Americans who preferred "red likker" to any pale-faced brandy.

Thus brandy vanished from the Sazerac to be replaced by whiskey (Handy always used Maryland Club rye), and a dash of brandy was added. Precisely when whiskey replaced brandy and the dash of absinthe added are moot questions. The absinthe innovation has been credited to Leon Lamothe who in 1858 was a bartender for Emile Seignouret, Charles Cavoroc & Company, a wine importing firm located in the old Seignouret mansion still standing at 520 Royal Street. More likely it was about 1870, when Lamothe was employed at Pina's restaurant in Burgundy street that he experimented with absinthe and made the Sazerac what it is today.

But this history delving is dry stuff, so let's sample a genuine Sazerac. We will ask Leon Dupont, now vice-president of the St. Regis Restaurant but for years one of the expert Cocktail mixers behind Tom Handy's original Sazerac bar, to make one for us. Here's how—and how!

1 lump sugar
3 drops Peychaud's Bitters
1 dash Angostura Bitters
1 jigger rye whiskey
1 dash absinthe substitute
1 slice lemon peel

To mix a Sazerac requires two heavy-bottomed, 3.5-ounce bar glasses. One glass is filled with cracked ice and allowed to chill. In the other a lump of sugar is placed with just enough water to thoroughly moisten it. The saturated lump of sugar is then crushed with a bar spoon. Add a few drops of Peychaud's bitters, a dash of Angostura, a jigger of rye whiskey, for while bourbon may do for a julep it just won't do for a real Sazerac. To the glass containing sugar, whiskey, and bitters several good sized lumps of ice must be added and all stirred with a spoon. Never use a shaker! Empty the first glass of its ice, dash in one or two drops of absinthe, twirl the glass and shake out the absinthe ... enough will cling to the sides of the glass to give the necessary flavor. Strain into it the mixture, twist a piece of lemon peel over it, but do not commit the sacrilege of dropping it into the drink. Some bartenders put a cherry in a Sazerac; very pretty but not necessary. That, ladies and gentlemen, is a Sazerac Cocktail—the appetizer New Orleans made famous. M-m-m-m! Let's have another, Leon![76]

With that bit of sage advice, and rather thirsty myself, I will conclude this article. Cheers.

76. Stanley Clisby Arthur, *New Orleans Drinks and How to Mix 'Em* (1937).

# DOWN TO THE SEA IN SHIPS

## HISTORY OF GIN AND PLYMOUTH GIN

### BY ANISTATIA MILLER

*The story of gin's origins begins with the history two nations united in wars against France and Germany since the sixteenth century. In its early heyday, gin was called "mother's ruin" — the drink of the working class masses who paid a penny per serving in London's gin palaces throughout the 1700s. But as legislation restricted who could produce and sell gin to the public and new inventions improved the final product, gin became the spirit of the elite, especially when it crossed paths with the officers of Great Britain's Royal Navy who took the spirit with them around the world. Anistatia Miller surveys gin's birth and rise to prominence in the world of Cocktails, focusing on the history of one of its most famous brands — Plymouth Gin.*

**W**HEN FRANCISCUS DE LA BOË (aka: Dr. Sylvius) recorded the healthful benefits of his juniper-laced tonic—*eau de vie de genievre*, eventually shortened to *jenever*—in 1565, did the Dutch Professor of Medicine at the University of Leyden have any clue that his aromatic grain spirit would reach sales in the US of 11 million cases in 2004[1] and become one of Great Britain's top five export industries, earning over £3 billion in 2002? Without a doubt, he did not. This harsh distillation of fermented barley, maize, rye and hops blended with oil of juniper berries evolved in less than two centuries into a smooth, aromatic spirit that stands as the central figure in such classic Cocktails as the Martini, the Gimlet, Ramos Gin Fizz, and of course, Gin & Tonic. But his promotion of *jenever*'s medicinal aspects did help bolster the image and popularity of what was to become known as gin.

Juniper berries—regarded as an antiseptic, diuretic, antiviral and detoxifier since Greek and Roman times—were especially favored by Europeans. These pungent berries gather from an evergeen shrub were notably used as a preventative against the bubonic plague. When the Black Death stormed across the Continent and the British Isles (1347-1350), people burned juniper incense, wore masks laced with juniper oil, and drank juniper elixirs (supposedly developed by Italian alchemists and monks) to ward off the disease, which claimed nearly a quarter of the population. Juniper was used as a flavoring and preservative in smoked meats, sausages, and other foods. By the six-

---

1. Adams Handbook Advance 2004.

teenth century, its appeal had broadened from valuable medicine to become a popular flavor.

The Dutch were world-class distillers by 1500. Books on the subject such as Hieronymous Brunschwig's *Kleines Distillerbuch* (1500) clearly illustrated that the Arabian art of distillation had taken hold in the Low Countries. By the time Dr. la Boë was stumping the benefits of his *jenever* in the treatment of stomach complaints and kidney ailments, its woodsy aroma and hops-laced flavor appealed to those who drank the tonic not only for its medicinal properties, but for its remarkable taste. Demand surpassed la Boë's ability to produce *jenever*. Bols—founded by Lucas Bols in 1575 and still in operation today—was only one of 200 *jenever* distillation houses established in Schiedam, near the port of Rotterdam, that made la Boë's tonic.[2] And it's no surprise that some say *jenever* was plentifully available by the late 1580s, when British troops first landed in the Netherlands to fight the Spanish during the Dutch War of Independence (1567-1609). The British gratefully drank drams of it to give them "Dutch courage" during battle.[3] The troops that came to fight during the Thirty Years War (1618-48)[4] similarly found their nerve drinking *jenever* and happily brought their taste for "gin" home to England.

As a medicinal tonic, *jenever* had made its way into British literature within a mere 20 years. Diarist Samuel

---

2. The unofficial *jenever* capital, Schiedam—a satellite of Rotterdam—was also home to Heinken, which produced produced Bokma Jonge, another form of jenever; also see www.holland.com/us/index.html?page=http://www.holland.com/us/geninfo/press/ideas/drank.html

3. Alan S. Dikty, "Gin—Origins and History", *American Distiller*, No.7, Apr 2002.

4. One of the great conflicts of early modern European history, the series of declared and undeclared wars pitted the Catholic Hapsburg Holy Roman Empire and their cousin on the Spanish throne against the German Protestant princes who were supported by the thrones of Denmark, Sweden, the United Provinces (Holland) and England. The battles shifted through the years from Bohemia and Austria to the Netherlands and up to Livonia. But when the French declared war against the Spanish Hapsburgs—engineered by Cardinal Richelieu—and allied themselves with Sweden, the fighting fronts centered on the Rhine, Bavaria, and the Netherlands.

Pepys wrote of taking "strong water made of juniper" for a case of colic he suffered on October 10, 1663.[5] But it was Great Britain's only Dutch monarch William of Orange,[6] who fostered not only the importation of *jenever* from his homeland, but the distillation of gin in England as well. (Some say that William believed gin was safer and healthier to drink because it was "boiled" or distilled unlike British water or milk.[7]) More likely, the king and queen had guaranteed a market for Dutch imported spirits after banning the importation of French brandy and levying high taxes on the importation of German spirits following their ascent to the throne: the Distilling Act of 1690 was the result of pent-up prejudice after the events of the Thirty Year War.

William's prohibition on imported spirits and fostering of local distillation through lowered taxes on the use of "good English corn" in gin production had an immediate effect. Daniel Defoe, author of *Robinson Crusoe*, seconded the king's edict, writing in 1713:

"Nothing is more certain than the fact that the ordinary production of grain in England is much greater than our people or cattle can consume. Because gin is made from grain, the distilling trade is one remedy for this disaster as it helps to carry off the great quantity of grain in such a time of plenty. In times of plenty and a moderate price of grain, the distilling

---

5 . Pepys wrote: "Up, and not in any good ease yet, but had pain in making water, and some course. I see I must take besides keeping myself warm to make myself break wind and go freely to stool before I can be well, neither of which I can do yet, though I have drank the other bottle of Mr. Hollyard's against my stomach this morning. I did, however, make shift to go to the office, where we sat, and there Sir J. Minnes and Sir W. Batten did advise me to take some juniper water, and Sir W. Batten sent to his Lady for some for me, strong water made of juniper." See Samuel Pepys, *The Diary of Samuel Pepys: A New and Complete Transcription*; edited by Robert Latham and William Matthews. (London: Bell, 1970).

6. Also known as William III of England or William Henry, this Dutch prince co-ruled England, Scotland, and Ireland along with his wife, Mary II, who was the Protestant daughter of the deposed King James II following the Glorious Revolution of 1688.

7. See "The History of Gin (and Tonic)" at www.bbc.co.uk/dna/h2g2/A2451386.

of grain is one of the most essential things to support the landed interest and therefore especially to be preserved."[8]

Numerous distilleries opened throughout the country. One example was Black Friars, which began as a Dominican monastery in 1431. Situated a few blocks from the port in Plymouth, the monastery flourished until the Reformation. In 1539, the monastery was dissolved as were monastic orders throughout the kingdom per Henry VIII's royal decree. The building then served as a marshalsea[9] and debtor's prison; as the first Non-Conformist meeting house in 1672; and as a billet for Huguenot refugees who emigrated to England during the 1680s. (It's reputed that the building's priory served as lodgings for some of the Pilgrim Fathers before they set sail for the New World in 1620.) According to a deed of sale dated November 12, 1697, the Black Friars had been converted into a "mault-house", where grain was malted, brewed, distilled and rectified (redistilled to purify and/or infuse herbs and spices rather than to increase the spirit's proof).[10]

By 1690, 500,000 gallons (or 210,000 cases) of gin were consumed in London alone. And in 30 years, approximately a quarter of London's houses and buildings were employed for the production and sales of nearly two million gallons (or 840,000 cases) of tax-free gin in 1721.[11] Between the 1720s and 1730s, nearly 7,000 gin palaces offered the city's population of a staggering half a million a place to imbibe a dram of gin for no more than a penny per serving. As Jessica Warner wrote in her book *Craze: Gin and*

---

8. See *The Best of Defoe's Review : An Anthology* , compiled and edited by William L. Payne. (New York : Columbia University Press, 1951).

9. A marshalsea was a court formerly held before the steward and marshal of the king's house to administer justice between the king's domestic servants.

10. Geraldine Coates, *Plymouth Gin: The Adventure* (Plymouth: Coates & Company, 2003).

11. Alan S. Dikty, "Gin—Origins and History", *American Distiller*, No.7, Apr 2002; Customs Library, Excise Revenue Accounts 1701-1751; and class.fst.ohio-state.edu/fst59701/lecture_10.htm.

*Debauchery in an Age of Reason:* "In 1700, the average adult drank slightly more than a third of a gallon of cheap spirits over the course of a year; by 1720 that amount had nearly doubled; and by 1729, the year when the first Act restricting sales of gin was passed, the number had nearly doubled again, to slightly more than 1.3 gallons [about 5 litres] per person. The figures include only the population fifteen years of age or older, although there were as yet no formal restrictions on minors' access to alcohol."[12]

Legal and illegal gin production rampaged as the major cities fell into a well-documented mass drunken stupor. Gin was the drink of working classes, who toiled in the factories that rose up during the Industrial Revolution, and the poor. Public outcries for temperance and prohibition were fueled by pamphlets such as *Distilled Liquors: the Bane of the Nation* (1736), which reported: "Everyone who now passes through the streets of the great city of London and looks into the gin shops must see, even in shops of creditable and wholesome appearance, a crowd of poor ragged people, cursing and quarreling with one another over repeated glasses of these destructive liquors. In one place not far from East Smithfield, a trader has a large empty room where, as his wretched guests get intoxicated, they are laid together in heaps, men, women and children, until they recover their senses, when they proceed to drink on, or having spent all they had, go out to find the means to return to the same dreadful pursuit."

But in Parliament, gin production was viewed as a trade not a public hazard. As the First Earl of Bath, William Pulteney, said in a speech to Parliament in 1736:

"Let us consider, Sir, that the gin trade has been carried on for about 100 years and that it has been very much encour-

---

12. Jessica Warner, *Craze: Gin and Debauchery in an Age of Reason* (Berkeley, CA: Publishers Group West, 2002).

aged by several acts of Parliament. No one could imagine that the trade is in itself detrimental to the health and welfare of the people. Accordingly, great numbers of his Majesty's subjects, especially within the last 40 years, have entered this business. There is not an inn, an alehouse, or a coffeehouse in the kingdom, but what owes a great part of its profits to the sale of gin. There are now multitudes of families in the kingdom who owe their chief if not their only support to the distilling, or to the sale of such liquor. They deserve the care and the consideration of the British House of Common. I cannot give my consent to any regulation which will put them out of the business to which they owe their chief support."

The first—and wholly ineffectual—Gin Act of 1736 was passed by Parliament and led to riots across the nation. In the great drinking hubs of London, Bristol and Plymouth, mock funeral processions mourned the death of "Madame Geneva." The act failed to regulate gin production or consumption. Six British port cities had become gin-producing centers: London, Bristol, Norwich, Warrington, Liverpool and Plymouth. And domestic consumption reached an all-time high of 2.2 gallons (about 8 litres) per person in 1743.

With the passage of the Gin Act of 1751, the three-decade-long "gin epidemic" and the proliferation of cheap spirits receded. Consumption sank to 1.2 gallons (about 4.5 litres) per person in 1752. Restrictions on who could produce and sell gin set in place in 1756 as well as the introduction of excise taxes on gin dropped the per capita to 0.6 gallons (2.27 litres).[13]

By the 1790s, enough legislation had been set in place and enforced that the days of cheap gin were over. Reputable businessmen began taking over the gin trade, offering consumers reliably distilled spirits that used more delicate flavorings and less sugar in their formulations than

---

13. Jessica Warner, *Craze: Gin and Debauchery in an Age of Reason* (Berkeley, CA: Publishers Group West, 2002).

their predecessors. Sir Robert Burnett, James Burroughs (Beefeater), Walter and Alfred Gilbey, Charles Tanqueray, and Gilbert and John Greenall were just a few of the new generation of gin distillers who made their mark at that time. Sir Felix Booth did so well with his particular formulation, he financed James Ross's arctic expedition in 1829. (The Boothia Felix Peninsula in Canada's Northwest Territories was named by Ross as thanks to his benefactor.)

Another distiller made his mark on the new gin trade, not in London, but in Plymouth. In 1793, a distiller named Mr. Coates joined the company of Fox & Williams, which had set up operations in the Black Friars Distillery in Plymouth and began producing Plymouth Gin. This Devonshire seaport city offered gin distillers two major opportunities for growth: an abundance of exotic ingredients and a major, local target audience—the Royal Navy.

Since 1211, the port's Barbican area had been a center for trade. The water-gate of the medieval castle that once protected the entrance to Sutton Harbor, the Barbican lent its name to the whole port area by Tudor times. As Britain's sphere of influence grew, so did the number of types of cargo that landed in Plymouth's Barbican: herbs and spices from the East, sugar from the West, citrus fruits from southern Europe. All the ingredients needed to make gin landed at the wharves, only a few blocks from the distilleries' doorsteps.

Plymouth became the Royal Navy's home port back in 1294, when Edward I assembled the first naval fleet during one of the numerous territorial wars between England and France. During Elizabeth I's reign, the buccaneer John Hawkins and circumnavigator Francis Drake set sail from Plymouth harbor, returning with treasures and tales of the New World. The Spanish Armada was defeated by the fleet sailing from Plymouth under the leadership of then-Admiral Francis Drake in 1588. William of Orange then assured the permanency of the relationship between Plymouth and the naval fleet when he founded the Naval Dockyard in Devonport in 1691.

In the years after Mr. Coates joined Fox & Williams to distill gin in Plymouth, the business grew. The Napoleonic Wars (1803-1815) contributed to its growth. The ordinary seamen who sailed under Admiral Lord Nelson received daily rations of beer and rum as they sailed into battle at Cape St. Vincent, Copenhagen, Tenerife, and Trafalgar. The officers of the Royal Navy drank gin—particularly Plymouth Gin—which they had undoubtedly acquired a taste for during their stays at home.

By 1820, Coates had become a senior partner of the flourishing enterpiseand the company name was changed to Coates & Company.[14] A mere five years later, legislation forced the evolution of the thriving business: distilleries were no longer allowed to distill spirit and rectify spirits into gin or any other beverage in the same location. Coates & Company chose to cease its fermentation and distillation operations to focus its attention on the rectification of gin.[15]

Another development altered the type of gin the company produced. In 1831, the Irish inventor Aeneas Coffey developed the column—or continuous— still. Coffey's still offered distillers an opportunity to efficiently create a purer base spirit that didn't need sugar and strong spices to mask unwanted congeners. Many producers formulated recipes that enhanced the main juniper aroma with drier flavors such as lemon, orange, orris root, angelica, car-

---

14. Geraldine Coates, *Plymouth Gin: The Adventure* (Plymouth: Coates & Company, 2003).
15. Ibid.

damom and coriander. Sugar was completely eliminated from the blend and dry gin was born.

All of these changes in production didn't seem to diminish the Royal Navy's appreciation for gin. Rather, continuous-still distillation and an enhanced recipe seemed to increase interest among naval officers who carried their gin rations around the world as the Empire reached its apex under Queen Victoria. Plymouth Gin followed the fleet to colonial ports far and wide, from the Caribbean to the South Seas. Coates & Company then instigated a new tradition that continues to this day. Every new vessel in the fleet was presented with a commissioning kit: a handsome wooden case containing glasses, a branded "glug-glug" jug in the shape of a fish, a bottle or two of Navy Strength Plymouth Gin, and a green-and-white flag known as a "Gin Pennant." Whenever and wherever a ship hoisted the pennant, it meant it was time to "come aboard for a drink".

Gin was more plentiful than potable drinking water on voyages. And naval surgeons took advantage of its availability to deliver healthful tropical disease preventatives such as anti-malarials and anti-scorbutics to the ship's officers. Stomach complaints and fatigue often plagued sailors headed into tropical regions. Angostura bitters—a formula introduced by Dr. J.G.B. Siegart in 1824—was considered to be the most effective cure. But the bitter tonic, a blend of 40 different herbs and spices, was unpalatable on its own. In 1848, one Royal Navy ship's surgeon added few drops of Dr. Siegart's bitters to a jigger of Plymouth Gin. Thus, the Pink Gin or "Pinkers" was born.

**PINK GIN**
2 dashes Angostura bitters
2 ounces Plymouth Gin
2 ounces water

Coat the glass with the bitters by swirling it in the glass. Then add
the gin and water until the liquid turns pink.

As the power of the British India East Company gave
way to the might of the British Raj, another popular way
to "take one's medicine" with gin was invented by officers
stationed in India—Gin & Tonic. Around 1825, the men
had discovered that one of the best ways to combat malaria
was to take quinine—a chemical compound found in cin-
chona bark. Quinine-laced tonic water[16] was no more easy
for most people to palate than Angostura bitters, so officers and colonists added gin make the preventative more
pleasing.

### GIN & TONIC
2 ounces Plymouth Gin
5 ounces Schweppes Indian Tonic Water

Fill a glass with ice. Pour in the gin and then gradually add the
tonic water. Garnish with a lime wedge.

Were these drinks popular? By 1850, Coates & Company was supplying over 1,000 barrels (23,000 cases) of
"navy strength"—57 percent alcohol by volume (abv) or
100° UK proof or 114° US proof—Plymouth Gin to the
Royal Navy each year. Alcoholic proof measures how much
ethanol, or "grain alcohol" an alcoholic beverage contains.
The proof number is twice the percentage of the alcohol
content measured by volume, at a temperature of 60 °F
(15.5 °C). Therefore, 80° proof equals 40 percent abv—
the remainder is 60 percent water. The proof system dates
back to when spirits were graded with gunpowder. If a pinch

---

16. Jacob Schweppes patented a process for infusing carbon dioxide into water
and a bottling system that retained the carbonation back in 1783. Shortly thereafter,
he and his partners moved their business from Switzerland to London, where they continued to sell their soda waters.

of gunpowder could be wetted with a solution of alcohol and water with and still ignite, the solution was "proven" to be at 100° proof, according to the British proof measuring method. According to the US measuring system, the "proven" number was found to be 57.15 percent alcohol or 114.30° US proof. With this "navy strength" gin on board, the fleet was assured they could drink *and* do battle without hindrance.[17] ✳

The Royal Navy's consumption of gin greatly enhanced gin's prestige among genteel Victorians. Ladies sipped glasses of gin infused with sloe berries and made gin-based punches for both male and female party guests. This increased demand convinced Coates & Company it was time to invest in a new copper continuous still, which was installed at Black Friars in 1855 and is still in use today.[18]

Since 1795, the Royal Navy had been stocking their ships with lemons, limes, and eventually, preserved lime juice as a preventative against scurvy, thanks to the insistence of Gilbert Blaine, a gentleman physician. But lemons and limes are not easy to digest on their own and spoil easily on long voyages. And so again, another gin Cocktail was reputedly created by a clever ship's surgeon, Sir Thomas D. Gimlette (*see Paul Clarke's article on the Gimlet in this volume*) sometime during the late 1870s.

### GIMLET
3 parts Plymouth Gin
1 part Rose's Lime Juice Cordial

Combine the gin and lime juice in a mixing glass and stir. Strain into a chilled cocktail glass. Garnish with a lime wedge.

---

17. See a definition of alcoholic proof in encyclopedia.laborlawtalk.com/Alcoholic_proof.

18. Gin rectification is much gentler on a still than distilling. The UK's whisky distilleries periodically replace their stills, but the Plymouth still is the oldest of its size in operation in England.

Gin and its relation to health in England went far beyond Cocktails created for their medicinal properties. In 1884, Plymouth Gin was awarded a medal at the International Health Exhibition, which was intended to bring healthy diet, hygiene and exercise to the minds of London's general populace. But by this time, that meant little to most gin aficionados. Cocktail's Golden Age (1880-1910) had taken hold in England and the Americas. And gin-based libations such as the Martini, Ramos Gin Fizz, Gin & It, plus the Gin Rickey were only a small handful of the drinks invented by bartenders of the day.

By 1896, Plymouth Gin was directly referenced in the earliest known recipe for a "dry Martini," appearing in Thomas Stuart's book *Stuart's Fancy Drinks and How to Mix Them*[19]:

### MARQUERITE
I dash orange bitters
two-thirds Plymouth Gin
one-third French Vermouth

Plymouth Gin sales went out the roof! By the 1900s, more than a 1,000 cases per week of an American export strength (44.5 percent abv) Plymouth Gin were being shipped to New York City alone. The brand represented the largest export segment of the UK gin market and was sold in 50 countries. Based on those sales, Plymouth was the number one gin brand in the world. Then came Prohibition.

The Volstead Act did not stop the importation of Plymouth Gin into the US. But it did require the company to affixed tax stamps on its bottles such as one, which stated: "Inventoried under Act of Congress, Oct. 3, 1917. UNI-

---

19. Thomas Stuart, *Stuart's Fancy Drinks and How to Mix Them* (original edition, 1896; New York: Excelsior Publishing House, 1904.)

VESRITY CLUB 1st District, Illinois." The company also offered a $100 reward to anyone who could provide evidence of any counterfeit Plymouth Gin being produced. (The company had filed injunctions against local Plymouth Gin "imitators" as far back as 1882 and 1888.)

Back at home, Plymouth or its only true competition at the time, Booth's, was the main ingredient in more than a quarter of the estimated 7,000 Cocktails that *Drinks and Drinking*[20] author John Doxat estimated were developed by Jazz Age barmen for the pleasure of the "Bright Young Things"—rootless rich kids and wealthy young widows disillusioned by the First World War, who inhabited London and Paris during the 1920s and 1930s. Take, for example, the American Bar at the Savoy's Harry Craddock, who created 27 Cocktails that specified the use of Plymouth Gin, including The Charlie Lindbergh, Gimlet, Pink Gin, the Million Dollar Cocktail, One Exciting Night, the Gene Tunney, and the Prohibition Cocktail:

### PROHIBITION COCKTAIL

2 ounces Plymouth Gin
2 ounces Lillet Blanc
one-half teaspoon apricot brandy
1 teaspoon orange juice

Shake and strain into a cocktail glass. Squeeze in a twist of lemon and discard.

Craddock's extensive work was memorialized in the first edition of *The Savoy Cocktail Book* in 1930, which is still considered to be one of great bibles of mixology. The fame of Craddock's famous book gained widespread popularity across the "pond" after Prohibition was repealed in 1933.

---

20. John Doxat, *Drinks and Drinking: An International Distillation* (London: Ward Lock, 1971).

Installed in 1855, this copper continuous still continues to be used to rectify Plynouth Gin to this day. (Photo courtesy of and ©2005 Jared Brown.)

By this point, Coates & Company had to protect its own good name at home once again. The firm had successfully deterred local imitators in the courts since the 1880s. But in 1933, the company filed a landmark case against a relative outsider—James Burroughs Ltd, makers of Beefeater's Gin. The company had attempted to market its own "Plymouth Gin" at its London distillery. Coates & Company won its case and a Geographic Designation (similar to an Appéllation Controleé) was placed in the law books, which stipulated that any gin called "Plymouth Gin" had to be produced within the ancient city walls of Plymouth, England.[21] Thus, Plymouth Gin became the first and only gin with a Geographical Designation.

Then came the Second World War...

The US, China and most of Europe experienced grain shortages during the 1930s. Great Britain's harvests also fell short of expectations. This forced gin producers like Plymouth to use cane sugar-based spirit for production by 1939. But even those weren't the darkest days the company experienced as the War Years emerged. Because the city was the Royal Navy's home, Plymouth's city centre and dock were relentlessly bombed during the Blitz of March and June 1941.[22]

Throughout the war lookouts were posted on the roof of Black Friars Distillery to watch for descending bombs. Unfortunately, one incendiary bomb struck the buildings, causing a severe fire that destroyed much of the company's written history and records. Townspeople and distillery workers formed a bucket brigade and doused the flames before they could spread to the distillery itself. When the smoke cleared over the embattled city, the Admiralty sent

---

21. From the document "Plymouth Gin: A Brief History".
22. Geraldine Coates, *Plymouth Gin: The Adventure* (Plymouth: Coates & Company, 2003).

a message to the entire fleet telling of the city's near decimation and the survival of the Black Friars Distillery.[23]

After the bombing of the distillery, the British officers in Malta offered any gunner who shot down an enemy plane or sank an enemy ship a bottle of Plymouth Gin.[24]

The continued rationing of grain and grain neutral spirit left Coates & Company unable to procure the high-quality base spirit it needed to rectify its gin even went the war ended. Its greatest supporter—the Royal Navy—had become so disheartened by the brand, it switched its loyalty to Horse's Neck. Brands such as Gordon's had established distilleries outside of Great Britain, so the balance of influence in the export market moved drastically away from Plymouth throughout the world. By 1946, grain rations had been lifted, but the company coffers were depleted. Coates & Company was forced to sell the business to entrepreneur J.C. McLaughlin in 1953.[25]

Plymouth Gin didn't completely disappear from the public eye during the dark years that followed. American author John S. Macdonald, created the detective character Travis McGee, who sipped Plymouth in nearly 20 novels beginning in 1957, revealing to readers a true obsession with the brand in books including *Purple Place for Dying*, *Quick Red Fox* and *Nightmare in Pink*.[26] Meanwhile, McLaughlin sold the company to Seagers Evans (owned by the US-based Schenley Industries) the next year. The new owners invested money into the distillery, but it also used it to make their own brands of gin and vodka to defray costs.

During the 1960s, Schenley imported the brand under the marketing lead of MD Dick "Bomber" Harris, who

---

23. Geraldine Coates, *Plymouth Gin: The Adventure* (Plymouth: Coates & Company, 2003).
24. Ibid.
25. Ibid.
26. Ibid.

began presenting Plymouth Gin commissioning kits to pres-tigious American yacht owners such as the Commodore of the St Francis Yacht Club in San Francisco. He didn't target the US Navy because the fleet was "dry" at sea. In 1966, Sir Francis Charles Chichester put Plymouth back on the world map when he drank Pink Gin made with the venerable spirit while he sailed solo around the world in his 53-foot yacht, the *Gipsy Moth IV*, from Plymouth to Sydney, Australia, in 107 days and tackled the 119-day return trip sipping the same libation. When asked what was the lowest point of his 226 days at sea, he replied: "when the gin ran out."[27]

But the marketing and public relations efforts didn't yield enough results for the American parent company. Schenley sold the brand along with other parts of its Long John portfolio to the British Whitbread PLC in 1975. Back in the hands of British owners once again, the brand still didn't regain the stature it had attained before the Second World War.

As MacDonald—in the guise of Travis McGee—wrote in 1974:

> At drinking time I left Meyer at the wheel and went below and broke out the very last bottle of the Plymouth Gin which had been bottled in the United Kingdom. All the others were bottled in the US. Gin People, it isn't the same. It's still a pretty good gin but it is not a superb, stingingly dry, and lovely gin. The sailor on the label no longer looks staunch and forth-right, but merely hokey. There is something self-destructive about Western technology and distribution. Whenever a con-sumer object is so excellent that it attracts a devoted following, some of the slide rule and computer types come in on their twinkle toes and take over the store, and in a trice they fig-ure out just how far they can cut quality and still increase market penetration. Their reasoning is that it is idiotic to

---

27. "Plymouth Gin to Sponsor Gipsy Moth IV," *IBI Magazine*, Feb 23, 2005.

make and sell a hundred thousand units of something and And Other Things
make a profit of 30 cents a unit, when you can increase the
advertising, sell five million units, and make a nickel profit
a unit. Thus the very good things of the world go down the
drain, from honest turkey to honest eggs to honest tomatoes.
And gin.[28]

Discouraged by low sales, Whitbread then purchased
a Plymouth competitor, James Burroughs Ltd, owners of
Beefeaters Gin, in 1982. Both brands continued to be neg-
lected as the worldwide drinking public turned its atten-
tions away from three-martini lunches to wine, beer, and
bottled water during the 1980s. The company pulled out
of the spirits business in 1991, selling both Beefeaters and
Plymouth to Allied-Lyons, which later became Allied
Domecq.[29]

The worst blow came when the new owners down-
graded Plymouth's base spirit from 40 percent abv to 37.5
percent abv; switched from grain to cane sugar once again;
and cheapened both the bottle and the label in an effort
to reduce losses in its investment. Production reached an
all-time low. The 50-person staff employed to produce Plymouth as well as the Seager's brands of gin and vodka during
the 1960s was reduced to a skeleton crew, who only worked
twice a year to produce 5,000 cases of Plymouth Gin.[30]
Exportation had reached the zero level and domestic sales
were anything but rewarding. Black Friars Distillery was
close to shutting down.

A change in consumer interest in Cocktails took place
during the mid-1990s. Martinis and other gin-based drinks
were being rediscovered by a twenty-something audience
of cocktailians fueled by a growing lounge culture and the

---

28. John Macdonald, *The Dreadful Lemon Sky* (Philadelphia: Lippincott, 1974).
29. Geraldine Coates, *Plymouth Gin: The Adventure* (Plymouth: Coates & Company, 2003).
30. Ibid.

emergence of a new breed of mixologists and Cocktail authors. Interest in gin was renewed in Great Britain and the US. And in 1996, a group of four private investors, headed by John Murphy, purchased the company from Allied Domecq.[31]

The spirit was reconfigured under the watchful eye of Head Distiller Sean Harrison. Grain neutral spirit replaced the inferior cane sugar base. Rectification was reset to 40 percent abv. And under the leadership of then-Managing Director Charles Rolls, production rose from 5,000 to 50,000 cases per year—with exports up eightfold—by 1997.[32]

The next year, Plymouth regained its visual presence with a return to its traditional label style, which features an illustration of the *Mayflower*. And the monk who appeared on labels dating back to 1882 reappears on the inside of the bottle, reviving the motto: "When his feet get dry, it's time for another bottle." Sean Harrison elevated the original strength to 41.2 percent abv because "it is a strength which holds all our seven botanicals perfectly without the alcohol burn evident in many stronger gins."[33]

Distribution deals with Seagram UK and an equity purchase by Vin & Spirits in the past few years have ensured Plymouth Gin's future. The brand is now exported to 20 countries around the world. Under Managing Director Nick Blacknell, the distillery produced 231,000 cases in 2004. The brand family was expanded to include not only its navy strength and original strength gins, the Black Friars Distillery has developed a true sloe gin, damson plum liqueur,

---

31. From the document "Plymouth Gin: A Brief History."
32. Geraldine Coates, *Plymouth Gin: The Adventure* (Plymouth: Coates & Company, 2003).
33. Ibid.

and a classic fruit cup all produced with the company's signature premium spirit.[34]

Other gins' histories parallel Plymouth Gin's story to some extent. However, none rose to such heights, fell to such lows and was so completely restored in the end. As a category, gin is unlikely to see a meteoric rise like vodka, but will undoubtedly continue to grow as consumers who have learned to appreciate Cocktails through vodka-based drinks seek out increasingly complex flavors. And as long as a core of drinkers consider a Gin Martini to be the only true Martini, a Gin & Tonic to be the ultimate civilized summer cooler, and Pink Gin to be the sailor's tipple, gin will always have a solid base market to sustain it while its producers court those new consumers.

---

34. Ibid.

# THE
# DEFINITIVE GUIDE
# TO SIMPLE SYRUP

BY DARCY S. O'NEIL

*Water and sugar should be a simple matter of combining two essential elements in equal portions until completely dissolved, right? Chemist-turned-mixologist Darcy O'Neil shows there is more science to the making of simple syrup than meets the eye.*

OW COULD A PRODUCT WITH such a "simple" name cause so much confusion? Well, the main reason is individual preferences. Some people like a super-sweet drink, others a bitter brew with the edge taken off. Just to make things a little more difficult, the original creator of the Cocktail may have his own special formula for simple syrup. That leaves us with no standards and no consistency, which can be bad. As a bartender what can you do?

Well the first step is to understand what sugar syrup is and how sugar plus water combine to make "simple syrup" or "gomme" (pronounced: "gum"). On a basic level, it's very simple: add sugar to water and we have syrup. But take a look a little deeper and you'll find out that chemistry and math play a significant role in the quest for the perfect Cocktail. Follow along and I'll break it down so it's easy to understand and even easier to put into practice.

To start, let's take a look at a common recipe for a 1:1 ratio simple syrup (v/v).[1] Basically, you take one part sugar and add it to an equivalent amount of water. If you are in a rush, you can warm up the mixture to increase the rate at which the sugar dissolves into the water. Generally, as long as you are working in a fairly warm area the sugar will dissolve on its own (cold process). *Voilá*, you now have basic simple syrup.

So that was simple. Now what? Well, for the sake of consistency, we need to look at things that can affect the character of your final product. For example, it has been

---

1. v/v means volume/volume, in some cases weight maybe used which would be w/w or even w/v

observed that heating up the sugar solution results in a lower quality product. Is this true? The answer is yes. But it's only partially true! First, the final product will not be of a lower quality, just have different characteristics. When table sugar (sucrose) is heated up, in the presence of water or acid, it breaks down into fructose and glucose through a process called hydrolysis. This resulting mixture is commonly called invert sugar. Glucose can also act as a reducing sugar, which increases the break down of sucrose to glucose/fructose.

So what changes you may ask? The first noticeable difference is that the viscosity of the liquid will change. Sucrose is, by far, the most viscose sugar in a simple syrup. The least viscose sugar is fructose, with glucose being slightly more viscose than fructose (the relative viscosity at room temperature is almost twice as high for sucrose than fructose). Ironically, a syrup made of sucrose will be thicker than a syrup made of fructose or glucose even when the latter contains more sugar by weight!

Secondly, the sweetness of the syrup will increase when sucrose is broken down into fructose and glucose. Medium invert sugar (50 percent sucrose, 50 percent glucose/fructose) has an increased sweetness of 20 percent to 30 percent, when compared to pure sucrose.

So the perceived quality loss is due to the lower viscosity and the change in sweetness. So the moral of the story is that if you overheat your mixture, you may end up with a different product than expected.

## FINAL VOLUME OF THE SYRUP

ost people notice that when adding the sugar to the water, the two combined parts do not add up to the expected volume (i.e., 1 cup sugar + 1 cup water ≠ 2 cups simple syrup). What is happening is that the sugar has dissolved into the water and is occupying the spaces between the water molecules, so the sugar is just filling up some empty space that was already there. In the end, it generally adds up to about 1.5 times the expected volume.

Why is this important? When bartending, the idea is to be as accurate as possible. And when using a syrup instead of crystalline sugar there is room for error. For example, one teaspoon of sugar does not equal one teaspoon simple syrup in the 1:1 ratio. If you know how much sugar is going into a drink, your drinks will be more consistent and that much better.

## HOW MUCH SUGAR SHOULD YOU USE?

So everyone who has bartended has heard a number of different recipes for the perfect simple syrup. However, not all simple syrups are created equal. The 1:1 ratio is probably the most common—and is a good starting point. But many people swear by the 2:1 or 3:1 and even 4:1 sugar-to-water syrups. The reality, when using these solutions, is that the amount of sugar going into a drink is unknown, which is bad for consistency. In most recipes that use crystalline sugar, it will call for a teaspoon or two. So if we want to measure a teaspoon or two of sugar in syrup form, how do we do that?

Warning: For those of you who have a phobia of math, hold on tight. You might want to pour a drink. But once you get through this, it will improve your consistency in drinkmaking and you will be that much more of a mixologist. Let's start with some basics facts to help us get started:

I cup of granulated table sugar = 210 grams (g)
I teaspoon of granulated table sugar = 4 grams (g)

So with this knowledge, we can determine how many milliliters of syrup will equal 1 teaspoon of sugar. For example, if we want 10 ml (a third of an ounce) of simple syrup to equal 1 teaspoon sucrose, we would take 400 g of sugar (roughly two cups) and dilute that to 1000 ml of water. (Please note: I do not mean add 1000 ml of water. I mean add water until the total volume of solution equals 1000 ml.) The best way to do this is to find a measuring cup that is marked for 250 ml. Find a container—clear bottles work nicely—and add 1000 ml of water to it. Make a mark where the water level is. Next, empty the water, add 400 g of sugar to the bottle and then add water slowly until it reaches the mark.[2] This is now a 400 g/L or 0.4 g/ml solution (i.e., When you pour 10 ml of this you will have 4 g or one teaspoon of sugar!). For a more concentrated solution, add 800 g of sugar to the bottle and dilute up to the mark. Now you have 1 teaspoon for every 5 ml of sugar syrup.

The old 1:1 ratio resulted in a solution that has about 6 g sucrose per 10 ml water. About 50 percent more sugar than an average teaspoon. The ratio of 2:1 sugar to water resulted in a solution that has about 9.5 g of sugar per 10 ml or 4.75 g per 5 ml.

So now we know what's going into our drinks. What's the best one to use? As long as we know how much sugar is going in we should be okay using which ever one suits your preference. However, there are two issues remaining. Some people believe dilution (aka: additional water in the

---

2. The easiest way to do this to to add about a cup of water to the sugar, mix, and then add this to the bottle.

drink) will make the Cocktail taste different as will the inconsistent free pouring of simple syrup.

The issue of dilution by extra water from the syrup is pretty small. For example, if we add 10 ml of the 1:1 syrup that will add an additional 6.5 ml of water to our drink. In a drink, let's say an Old Fashioned with 2 oz rye or 60 ml, with a glass full of ice, the drink liquid may total 100 ml in volume. Therefore the 6.5 ml of water from the sugar syrup is only 6 percent of the Cocktail. That isn't a significant change, especially when the ice continues to melt, further diluting your drink.

Here's an Old Fashioned recipe for you to use:

### OLD FASHIONED COCKTAIL
2 ounces rye whiskey
1 cube sugar
2 dashes Angostura bitters
one half of an orange slice

Muddle orange, sugar, bitters together until the sugar is mostly dissolved. Fill glass with ice, then add the whiskey. Garnish with a maraschino cherry, and an additional orange slice.

As for the error from a free pour of simple syrup, the sugar content of the drink can become significantly higher, especially with a 2:1 or greater solution. For example, one sugar cube equals one teaspoon or 4 g. In a 2:1 syrup you need to pour about 4 ml to equal a teaspoon of sugar. If you free pour and you do 10 ml you've doubled the sugar content of the recipe. That is an error of roughly 100 percent. Now if you're using 3:1 or 4:1 you will have to be even more accurate, which is time consuming and a consistency nightmare.

So which is more important, 6 percent flavourless water or twice as much sugar when making a drink? I'm going to go with the fact that too much sugar can be a bad thing and a little extra water won't adversely affect the drink, especially when the drink is built with ice. Now I'm not saying don't use 2:1 simple syrup. In fact, I'll be providing a recipe that's very close to this later on. I'm just saying when you do use it, measure it accurately. Your clients will appreciate it.

## MAKING THE PERFECT SIMPLE SYRUP

**N**ow for the big question: What makes the perfect simple syrup? For the answer to this question, we will have to look at our main ingredients, the preparation, and the concentration of our final product. First, let's take a look at our three main sugars—glucose, fructose and sucrose—and their unique characteristics.

## THE INGREDIENTS

**G**lucose (corn syrup) is the most important sugar from a biological standpoint, Basically, without glucose we could not function. Glucose will increase your energy levels rapidly but all it is also metabolized quickly.

Glucose is less sweet than sucrose—about three quarters the sweetness of sucrose. Also, it has a high glycemic index (100 on a scale of 100), which means that this type of sugar is absorbed very rapidly into your system. Basically, it results in the sugar high, the sugar crash and bad hangovers. It does play one very important role in sugar syrups, though. Glucose helps prevent re-crystallization of sucrose. If added in a small amounts, your syrup will be more stable. Add it as about 10 percent to 15 percent of your sugar measure (i.e., 2 cups of sugar would require 0.25 cup corn syrup).

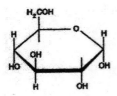

Fructose is a common sugar found in fruits and is about 1.8 times sweeter than sucrose. Many fruits are high in this sugar and can be found in its pure form in health food stores. Fructose is not as easily digested as glucose or sucrose. Humans cannot live on fructose alone. Fructose has a low glycemic index (22/100), which is good for people who drink very sweet drinks; want to spend a long time out drinking; or are diabetic. Fructose also enhances fruity flavors in drinks. So it can be beneficial in making a flavorful drink. Too much fructose can leave an aftertaste. So it is not recommended as a complete replacement for sucrose.

Sucrose is a disaccharide (two sugars) that is made of one glucose molecule and one fructose molecule. Sucrose is easily absorbed into your system and has a high glycemic index (64/100). This is the most common type of sugar and is the base for our simple syrup.

For our primary recipe this is what we will be using:

400 g of sucrose (roughly 2 cups table sugar)
and 50 g of glucose (0.25 cup corn syrup).

## PREPARATION

To make our simple syrup, add 2 cups of water to a pan and bring it to a simmer. A good temperature is about 50°C (122°F) to 60°C (140°F) or the point where it's just slightly too hot to put your finger in for more than a few seconds. This temperature will minimize the conversion of sucrose to fructose and glucose. But will be fast enough for convenience. Once the water is up to temperature, add your sugars and leave the heat on for about 30 seconds. Then, remove the pan from the heat and stir until all the sugar is dissolved. Let the solution cool down. Then add it to the bottle with a 1000 ml mark on it. Fill the bottle up with water to the 1000 ml mark and shake.

For the cold processing method you would just add the sugar and water to the bottle and shake, leaving a little air in the bottle to allow a vigorous shake. Then you just top up with water as before to get the required concentration.

## CONCENTRATION
## OF OUR FINAL PRODUCT

Now you have sugar syrup that has roughly 1 teaspoon of sugar per 10 ml or per a third of an ounce. For convenience, a one-ounce shot has 1 tablespoon of sugar in it. So what is the ratio of sugar to water? Well it works out to be roughly two parts sugar to three parts water.

If you want a more concentrated syrup, try the following recipe. This will result in a 1 teaspoon sugar = 1 teaspoon solution.

Combine 3.5 cups sucrose (granular table sugar) plus 0.5 cup glucose (corn syrup). Add one cup of water and dissolve all the sugar. (You may need to heat the mixture a little longer to bring the sugar into solution. But keep it low and do not boil.) Pour this mixture into your 1000 ml-marked bottle and top it up to the mark with water and then shake. You now have sugar syrup that has 8 g of sugar per 10 ml or 1 teaspoon of sugar per teaspoon of simple syrup.

### ONE TEASPOON SUGAR / 10ML
2 cups granular sugar
0.25 cup corn syrup

In a pot, add two cups of water and heat to approximately 60°C (140°F). Once the temperature has been reached add the corn syrup and sugar to the pot and continue to heat for about 30 seconds. Remove the pot from the heat source and allow to cool. Pour solution into bottle and fill with water to the 1 litre mark with water.

### ONE TEASPOON SUGAR / 5ML
3.5 cups granular sugar
0.5 cup corn syrup

In a pot, add two cups of water and heat to approximately 60°C (140°F). Once the temperature has been reached add the corn syrup and sugar to the pot and continue to heat for about two minutes. Remove the pot from the heat source and allow to cool. Pour the solution into the bottle and fill with water to the 1 litre mark with water.

## THINGS TO TRY

For the adventurous, try working with different ratios of sugars. Try adding a 0.25 cup of fructose in place of 0.5 cup sucrose. Then try it with fruit drinks to see if there is an improvement in flavor. You can also make invert sugar by boiling your sugar solution for 20 to 30 minutes. To speed up the process add a teaspoon or two of citric acid (available in the canning section of your grocery store).

## CONCLUSION

There is nothing better than a well-balanced drink. A good bartender will be accurate with his or her measures and know what's going into the drink. A consistent drink is the best product a bar can offer. Take a look a McDonald's™, and you'll realize that consistency is how it became the number one fast-food restaurant in the world.

From a financial perspective, the volume of your drink may increase slightly without any additional cost or flavor change. And the flavor of your drinks will be consistent with reduced errors. Your bar won't have to suffer from overly sweet drinks, which can decrease a client's desire for another drink or possibly losing that customer alltogether, because that drink didn't meet to up anticipated standards.

# TWENTY-FIRST CENTURY COCKTAILS

## THE NEW FRONTIER

### BY AUDREY SAUNDERS

*To leap into the future of Cocktails and create your own sig-nature drinks, you need to master the classics so you can build from a solid foundation. A well-known proponent of the classics, Audrey Saunders presents her own personal voice of the Cocktail's future, going from the bar to the kitchen and discovering new elements to incorporate into modern classics.*

**T**HESE ARE WONDERFUL TIMES in which to be a bartender. There's an enormous amount of experimentation happening on the global scene, with creative energy stemming from many different, directions. Aside from the desire to refine and perfect classic Cocktails, bartenders are now looking to hone and advance their skills—and taking a lot of direction from the kitchen and the culinary scene at large.

In the last couple of decades, we have witnessed restaurants becoming the new theatre, with chefs taking on starring roles. Cuisines fused with obscure ingredients emerged, and the "scientific kitchen" bloomed. With all of that going on, it is really no wonder that the crossover from the kitchen to the bar took place. Curious bartenders began collaborating with their chefs. The ingredients— previously exclusive to the kitchen—began showing up in Cocktails. It was at this point that the bar began to raise itself to another level. And it was no surprise either, as it was almost expected. When dining at a two- or three-star restaurant, one would naturally hope—and assume—that the Cocktails coming from the bar would be on par with the kitchen as well. As the bar is many times the first stop to the dining experience in a restaurant, it is a wonderful opportunity for bartenders to get creative, and show off their own talents.

There are a plethora of mediums available to us, right at our very fingertips. Bartenders are now shopping for their ingredients in the same specialty stores that chefs do, in the hopes that they will discover something that will bring their Cocktails to new levels, with different, added dimensions.

## FROM CLASSIC FOUNDATIONS
## TO MODERN MOVEMENTS

**W**hy stop with the perfection of a classic Cocktail when we have the option to tinker with it? I'm always trying to see if I can somehow build a better mousetrap, or put a fun twist on an old classic. To younger generation, classic Cocktails can be perceived as a little outdated and a bit dusty. But if you take a great old drink and put a modern twist on it, it can become fresh again. And it's that very freshness that has the ability to stimulate interest from the younger generation. A modern version of an old-school drink can also stir interest in the drink's origins (and sampling the original version becomes a possibility as well) thus becoming an in-through-the-out-door propagation of the classics.

But forget of all that for the moment. What I'm really trying to do right now is woo you a little, so you will think with an open mind as I begin to talk about the world beyond classic Cocktails as we know them. Don't get me wrong, I am truly an old-school girl at heart. But I've got a split personality that continually pulls me into the twilight zone of Cocktails, and I want to share some of that with you. Got a comfort level yet?

## CULINARY COMPONENTS AND THEIR
## RESPECTIVE ROLES IN COCKTAILS

**A**ll kidding aside, we now have a multitude of tools at our disposal which enable us to redefine Cocktails we know them: the ability to give them more depth and complexity than we've ever imagined. Let's look to the kitchen for a minute. What do we consider the components of a balanced dish to be?

One which encompasses sweet, sour, bitter, salty and these days, *umami*—considered to be the apex of "flavor perfection; ripened deliciousness." Why not take these media availed to us from cooking and convert them into liquids for use in Cocktails? These same components also exist in Cocktails, with the addition of "strong" (the base spirit), yet not necessarily all in the same glass.

Hopefully, I don't need to use this forum to preach about the importance of fresh ingredients; we agree about that, right? Let's delve into the various components of cuisine and how they translate into the world of Cocktails. You'll find that the majority of modern-day Cocktails being created by today's bartenders are primarily sour-based. We already understand the concept of combining fresh lemon or lime juice, a sweetening agent (i.e., simple syrup, triple sec, etc.), along with a spirit. *Voilà!* It's a sour! Yet an added bitter element such as Angostura, Peychauds or Orange Bitters serves a couple of different functions. Bitters can "dry down" the overall sweetness in a drink. It can also "round out" and tie flavors together.

And just exactly what does that mean? Many people are under the impression that bitters make a drink "bitter." In reality, they do just the opposite. They soften the harsh edges in a spirit and add a wonderful level of depth and complexity to a previously "flat-tasting" drink. Just a dash or two can work wonders in an overly-sweet Cocktail, helping to restore balance. I find them to be an indispensable part of the bar and wish that more bartenders would experiment with them. Think of Angostura as the bitters that contains some of the "holiday" spices, such as clove, cinnamon and allspice, among other ingredients. Peychaud's Bitters has a wonderful anise undertone and goes very well in many different Cocktails, especially whiskey-based ones. Try dashing it over vanilla ice cream to see what it tastes like: the sugar and cream in ice cream help to tame the intensities of the ingredients, making it easier to distinguish the flavors. You can also put a few dashes right in the center of your palm, and then rub your hands together. Now smell your palms. The heat from your hands will help to release the aromatic oils.

We love salt on french fries. That same element will boost and sharpen a drink as it does for the Margarita and the Salty Dog. Many chefs use salt not only in their savory dishes, but in a majority of their desserts as well. We consider the "strong"—the primary spirit—in a Cocktail much like the main attraction in a show; comparable to the focal component in a food course such as meat, fish or chicken. When we see that these common elements exist in both food and beverage, there's no reason why we shouldn't be treating the preparation of Cocktails with more of a culinary approach. And the more we focus on these similarities, the better our Cocktails can become.

But as with food, there is much more involved than just these basic components. Chefs further enhance their dishes with herbs and spices. So with a little out-of-the-box thinking, let's forge ahead and contemplate that direction with Cocktails.

## HERBS

We already work with mint. These days, the Mojito has become as much of a bar staple as the Cosmopolitan. The varying methodologies of mint alone in a classic Julep stirs debate. To muddle or not to muddle, that is the question. But aside from classic spearmint, we have so many other wonderful variants to choose from! Mint comes in a number of assorted flavors including chocolate, apple, pineapple and lime. Even more fun can be had with other assorted herbs such as lemon verbena, lemon thyme, rosemary, lavender, anise hyssop, bay laurel, chamomile and scented geranium. All of these lovely herbs are only a grocery- or greenmarket-purchase away. Limitless flavor combinations await us. All we need to do is just take the plunge. I can't wait for summer when I can already envision the flavor of fresh anise and hyssop being muddled with bourbon, fresh peaches and lemon wedges. Yum!

## SPICES

Let's also take a look inside the kitchen pantry. How about the use of spices? Okay, sure. A light dusting of freshly-grated nutmeg is fabulous on top of a Rum Punch. But how can we take dry spices one step further? By liquefying them. We've already been invaded by a plethora of vodka-based fruit infusions. So let's take our lead from there. The creation of fruit infusions has become pretty basic math for a lot of bartenders. And for the uninformed, directions on how to make them are only a mouse-click away with thousands of recipes available on the Internet. We have the ability to create spice infusions and tinctures as well to incorporate into our Cocktails. Something as simple as adding a few dashes of liquid cinnamon or pepper can completely transform existing Cocktails as we know them into Cocktails with much more vibrant flavor.

Here's how old this idea is. The 1887 version of "Professor" Jerry Thomas, *The Bartenders Guide* (reprints available from Vintagebook Press), has the "Here's How" on page 119. Therein are the recipes for various tinctures made with clove, cinnamon, cardamom and allspice. The old adage, "Everything that's old is new again," holds true. Products have become so simplified; so pre-squeezed, pre-mixed, and pre-flavored, that we've forgotten just how to utilize basic ingredients. I believe that the use of spices in cocktails is an idea that's time has returned. Here is the recipe for the "Professor" Thomas' clove tincture, which can easily translate to this day and age:

### TINCTURE OF CLOVES

Take I pound of cloves; warm them over a fire until quite hot ; put them quickly into a jar, pour on them I gallon 95 percent alcohol, cover them airtight, and let them stand I0 days. Draw off into bottles, and cork close.

And here's a modern-day recipe, which easily translates into a smaller batch of concentrated tincture:

### TINCTURE OF CLOVES

I ounce whole cloves
8 unces vodka (minimum 80° proof)
Quickly sauté cloves in a dry pan over a low heat for approximately 5 minutes, allowing them to release their aromatic oils. Add the cloves to the vodka; cover and seal for one week. Siphon off the clove-infused vodka and utilize in a dasher or a dropper bottle. Another good option is to purchase a small mister, which allows you to spray a thin coat on the inside of a glass, before adding in a Cocktail.

Experimenting with a variance of different spices will allow us to take our Cocktails to new heights.

## ADDING AROMA TO COCKTAILS

We should also think about following our nose. We have already established the five basic elements of taste in food. But it has been written that the average person is capable of detecting over 2,000 different scents! There is a new trend on the culinary scene that brings attention to the concept of scenting food, so why not create scented Cocktails? When you were a kid growing up, do you remember the simple pleasures of the "scratch-'n'-sniff"? You loved them simply because they gave us the opportunity to use your olfactory.

So just how do we go about accomplishing that? If used under proper direction, trace amounts of pure essential oils and hydrosols can be diluted into syrups and spirits (and the label should read "Only 100 percent pure essential oil", not just "100 percent essential oil." The word "only" is the key, here). Once properly diluted, we can incorporate them into Cocktails by utilizing a mister or a dropper, adding aroma.

Hydrosols? What are hydrosols? Like orange flower and rosewater, they are the scented, nutrient-filled waters that are left over once a flower—or plant, root, bark, needle, leaf or branch—has been distilled and its essential oil has been removed. A book that I thoroughly enjoyed reading is *Aroma* by Mandy Aftel and Daniel Patterson. They assert that if used properly, these scented oils and waters could not only transform existing cuisine from good to great, but would automatically link a powerful connection to emotion and memory as well. Let's think about how that could translate into the world of Cocktails.

Again, we've already established sweet, sour, salty, bitter and strong in Cocktails. But if we add aroma into the equation, we then have the ability to create Cocktails that can "transport" the drinker to another plane. To ingrain a memorable experience through aromatic recollection? It's already a fact. We love the wafting aroma of an apple pie in the oven. The perky nosegay of a Julep arouses our senses. Sound bizarre? You bet. But I guarantee to you, that aroma will eventually be incorporated into "new frontier" Cocktail concepts. How about a scratch-'n-sniff patch that gives you an idea of how a particular spirit will smell or taste? Why not?

## THE ADDITION OF TEXTURE
## INTO COCKTAILS

We are witnessing the rebirth of texture in Cocktails, as well. Some bartenders are now taking their lead from Ferran Adria, master chef of Spain's culinary laboratory El Bulli. Adria incorporates gelatin-based, flavored foams into many of his dishes. And now we see them being worked into Cocktails in order to replicate that same texture. Think of foam as the cloud incarnate, for a tactile experience. Ever wonder what a cloud feels like? Well, they don't feel fluffy by any means. (As an ex-skydiver, I can tell you that they're pretty wet and soggy.) Yet, we still like the idea of that fluffy texture. Foam satisfies our yearning for edible texture by encapsulating a flavor in the lightest, airiest possible form. Its idea is really nothing new; we have been aerating eggs into drinks for their texture for centuries. The only difference, now, is the progression from eggs to gelatin. From the Flip—a colonial specialty—to a Yard of Flannel to the New Orleans-born Ramos Gin Fizz; both eggs and gelatin offer very similar, foamy textures.

### RAMOS FIZZ
2 ounces London dry gin
1 ounce heavy cream
1 egg white
one-half ounce fresh lime juice
one-half ounce fresh lemon juice
three-quarters ounces simple syrup (1 to 1 sugar to water)
2-3 drops orange flower water
Soda water, preferably from a siphon
Measure all ingredients into a mixing glass. Shake long and hard. for at least one minute to emulsify egg white and cream, and strain into a Collins glass. Top with approximately 2 ounces of soda water. No garnish.

If used properly, the addition of foam as a component can be a wonderful juxtaposition in a Cocktail. I've sampled a dear friend's variation of a Gin Fizz topped with lemongrass foam, which was absolutely heavenly. Another friend tells me he's created individual Gin & Tonic jellies, which sounds like a real hoot for a party. Finally, an adult version of the jelly shot. How about classic Martini jellies sharing the same plate with the olives? Hors d'oeuvres, anyone? Granted, they are not every day indulgences, but the work going on out there becomes more fascinating by the minute, and it's thrilling to witness the experiments in progress. Remember *The Jetsons* cartoon series, when we chuckled at the thought of tablet-sized meals? One day someone will perfect a Gin & Tonic that comes in a tablet, and fizzes up; it's only a matter of time.

## WORKING WITH TEA

While we're at it, let's touch on tea. Tea is not only one of the most uncomplicated media to use, it's also one of the most consistent. The flavor profile of fruit infusions can be irregular: fruit flavor varies from crop to crop, so the outcome of this week's infusion can definitely differ from last week's batch. This can frustrate as we look for flavor consistency in our recipes. And with seasonal fruit, availability also can become an issue. The wonderful aspect of tea is that it's not only consistent in its flavor profile, but it's also available year round. Infusing a few spoonfuls of tea into a bottle of spirit for just a couple of hours is an extremely quick and efficient way to create a new flavor profile, and its complexity can contribute an enormous amount of depth to a cocktail. There are also a plethora of flavors unique to tea that you don't normally have access to in the produce section. We rarely, if ever, see the bergamot citrus fruit available here on the eastern seaboard. But its entrancing, heady aroma is easily accessible through Earl Grey tea. A Chai blend is a warming mix of sweet spices, which include cinnamon, clove, cardamom and pepper (the spice mix is referred to as garam masala in India) which is generally blended with black tea. A jasmine floral note in tea is completely intoxicating. Here is a basic recipe guideline for a general tea infusion:

### RECIPE FOR A BASIC TEA INFUSION
1 tablespoon of loose tea of your choice
8 ounces of the spirit of your choice (minimum of 80 proof)
Put the spirit in a glass bottle that has a cap and add the tea. Cap bottle and shake well. Allow the infusion to sit at room temperature for 2 hours, shaking and tasting periodically to see how rapidly the flavor is developing. After 2 hours, strain off the infusion through a paper coffee filter. Do not squeeze the tea leaves: doing this can release additional unwanted tannins into the infusion, which may not be desirable. If your infusion reaches the desired flavor in a shorter amount of time, then simply strain it off.

Half the fun of working with tea is discovering what its affinities are through experimentation: which teas pair with best with which spirits.

Tea is an area that I like to incorporate the foaminess of an egg white into.

Fruit and herb *tisanes* are chock-full of bright, easy flavor—yet black tea, red tea, assam, darjeerling and other teas have real backbone depending on the varying levels of tannins. (A *tisane* is the French word for an herbal infusion that doesn't contain any tea leaves.) I have found that incorporating an egg white into a tea-based Cocktail softens the intensity of the tannins, much the same way milk added to traditional, non-alcoholic tea does. Yet the egg white rounds out the tannic edges without coating your taste buds with the unnecessary dairy fat of milk or cream.

Again, it's nothing new—we've merely created an updated version of the Pisco Sour by having infused it with tea. Here's an example of building onto a classic foundation:

### RECIPE FOR A TEA-BASED "SOUR" WITH THE ADDITION OF AN EGG WHITE

0.75 ounce fresh lemon juice
1 ounce simple syrup (1 part sugar to 1 part water)
1.5 ounces tea-infused spirit
1 small egg white

Measure all ingredients into a mixing glass. Add ice, shake well to a 10-second count and strain into a chilled cocktail glass.

Try a side-by-side comparison: prepare the tea-based sour both with *and* without the egg white to understand the distinction of it's role.

## MASTERY OF AND RESPECT FOR THE CLASSIC FOUNDATIONS

There is lots of fun to be had in recipe development. All in all, it is even more important to have an understanding of a particular medium or methodology before you call it a day and the liquids in your shaker become your finished product. You don't become a mixologist just because you utilized some obscure ingredients in a drink and it seems "cool": real understanding and mastery comes into play with the perfection of such three-ingredient drinks as the Negroni, the Sidecar, the Margarita and the Sazerac. It's another one of those drinks which 99 percent of the time is served much too sweet.

Mastery of these drinks is part of the understanding of true balance. Just like you need a driver's license before you can get behind the wheel of a car, you should know exactly what each one of the ingredients you're working with taste like, and how they interact with each other in the mixing glass.

Experimentation is a wonderful opportunity to open up the mind and stimulate further thinking. Yet to offer the general public weird Cocktails with obscure ingredients is not only unfair, it's also just plain silly if the drink doesn't taste good. People are spending their hard-earned money at a bar. And at today's Cocktail prices, they shouldn't have to pause and decide whether or not they actually like the taste of something. That satisfaction should be instantaneous and gratuitous. The ideas should make sense. And the flavors should all balance together in complete harmony. Balance: There's that "B" word again. And with that said, I'll have an Old Fashioned, please.

# The LONG and WINDING ROAD

### RESEARCHING THE HISTORY CHAPTER
### FOR *THE JOY OF MIXOLOGY*

BY GARY REGAN

*For the average person, the idea of spending days, weeks, even months hovering over old books, the historical documents of a business, and the biographies of US Presidents is as exciting a prospect as chartered accountancy or actuarial work for an insurance firm. Gary Regan's account of his adventure into historical research for his book* The Joy of Mixology *proves that this road is, in truth, a riveting and eye-opening journey.*

**I**T TOOK ME YEARS TO GET A CONTRACT to write *The Joy of Mixology* (New York: Clarkson N. Potter, 2003): simply a case of not being able to find any editor out there who wanted to allow me to write what I wanted to write, how I wanted to write it. I got lots of letters and e-mails to the effect of, "If you could cut out these three chapters, and add one about how to gauge how much ice people need for parties of 10, 25, 50, and 100 people we might be interested...." Fascinating, I thought, and went on to the next publisher.

I was very close to signing one deal with an editor who my wife Mardee and I had worked with previously, a guy who was ready to let me write the book that was in my heart, but at the last minute his publishing house was involved in a merger, so I held back, fearing the worst. The worst happened. He lost his job. There's nothing quite so bad as writing a book for an editor who acquired your contract by default. The new editor assigned to the project just couldn't give a damn. Still, though, God was looking out for me. After She thought I'd sweated enough, I think she sent Roy Finamore, my editor at Clarkson N. Potter, to negotiate for my manuscript. The only thing that Roy wanted changed was that he wanted a bigger book than I'd proposed. He got it. I love Roy Finamore.

After writing *The Book of Bourbon and Other Fine American Whiskeys* (Shelburne, VT: Chapters Publishers, 1995) with Mardee I knew that researching the history chapter for my mixology book would be the fun part of my assignment. That turned out to be very true indeed. I harked back to the early 1990s when we first started to visit Kentucky where we met a certain Mike Veach, then archivist for a company called United Distillers, an entity that's now part of Diageo, the world's largest beverage company. Mike, an affable guy who we're still in touch with, simply handed over a set of floppy disks (remember floppy disks?), saying that they probably contained most of the historical facts we needed. He was right, to a point. They proved to be a great this doesn't make sense—a great point? No, it was a great jumping-off point. jumping-off point, with bulleted factoids for just about every bourbon under the sun. They also guided us on ways in which to collect more information.

Most files detailed the history of one brand of bourbon in note form, complete with references to tell us where Mike had found the information so we could check it. Some, though, gave historical data on more than one brand, especially when one family—the Browns of Old Forester fame, for example—had split up somewhere along the road, and brought us a few different brands of whiskey—J.T.S. Brown Bourbon being the not-quite-so-successful whiskey that was marketed by an off-shoot of the Brown family.

We took the files gratefully from Mike and added to them as we went along, getting more details from books referenced in Mike's timelines and from extra pieces of information gathered individual companies and other books on the subject.

A typical timeline looked something like this:

### J W Dant History

1836

Joseph W. Dant fashions a still out of a large Popular tree log and begins to distill whiskey at Dant's Station Kentucky (*Spirits*, [Filson Club, 1936]).

J W Dant grew his own grain and hand picked the choicest grain for his whiskey and then made his own cooperage (*Spirits*, [Filson Club, 1936]).

J W Dant had seven sons (including J B Dant of Yellowstone) who all were in the distilling industry (*Spirits*, [Filson Club, 1936]).

1854
J B Dant makes the first barrel of Yellowstone (*Spirits*, [Filson Club, 1936]).

1870
J W Dant builds a modern distillery at Dant's Station (*Spirits*, [Filson Club, 1936]).

1896
Dant distillery is incorporated (*Spirits*, [Filson Club, 1936]).

George Dant begins to study distilling under his father and brothers at the Dant disillery (*Spirits*, [Filson Club, 1936]).

George W Dant is the secretary and treasure for the new company. He continues to work for the company until it is closed during Prohibition (*Spirits*, [Filson Club, 1936]).

1911
The Mida's Financial Index, 1911, list the Dant Distillery as Dy. No. 169, 5th Dist. Dant, KY. with a capital value of $30,000 to $40,000.1

and so on and so forth. Once we had files on every brand we intended to cover in the book, we then had to integrate them into one huge file so we could look at any given year and know what was going on with near-as-damn-it every whiskey producer in America, and there we had the backbone of the history chapter. Then the fun began. To flush out the chapter it was necessary to read biographies, and books on social history.

We read a few books on US President Abraham Lincoln, for instance, and Ulysses S. Grant, too, became a subject of interest when we learned about the scandal of the Whiskey Ring (1874-1876), involving tax skimming that was seemingly going on within Grant's staff. Coming from the UK, I knew little about American history: save for the fact that the USA beat the heck out of us in the 1700s. After researching this chapter, though, I had a clear view of the past 300 years in the New World—all of it was tied to whiskey, though…

## JOY OF MIXOLOGY

There was no Mike Veach to help me with the history chapter of *The Joy of Mixology*, but Mike had taught me well. After *The Book of Bourbon* was put to bed, every time I bought a new book about booze of any sort—spirits, Cocktails, beers, wines, etc.— I added any information I found interesting to a similar sort of timeline: this one governed by the title of each book rather than the brand name of an individual whiskey. So when it came time to write the history chapter for my new baby, I already had the backbone of the piece. All I had left to do was read, read, read. It was time to spend money on antiquarian books. Boy was this fun.

Many of my favorite facts included in this chapter came from books that you might not think about reading when researching the history of Cocktails and mixed drinks. *Billy King's Tombstone*, by C. L. Sonnichsen, for instance, details life in Tombstone, AZ—it's not a tome about a tomb. There, I read with glee about a woman known as Mrs. Sleepy, so named simply because she was the wife of a Tombstone gambler with the nickname of Sleepy Tom. Mrs. Sleepy was "a big, buxom, good looking woman. …In dress she lived up to her role, startling the natives with flowing robes and velvet caps with gold tassels. In one point she was strictly orthodox; she drank large quantities of whiskey, like everyone else." Mrs. Sleepy didn't make it into the book, but I sure did enjoy learning about her antics.

There were also plenty of books that were fairly obvious to my needs. Anything concerning the seedy underbelly of anywhere on the face of the earth, for instance, was bound to contain drinking scenes. And Herbert Asbury, author of *Gangs of New York* seemed to know the seedy underbellies of most big cities in the USA, so once I found copies of his out-of-print books about New Orleans, and San Francisco, as well as his *The Great Illusion: An Informal History of Prohibition*. Asbury was one-stop shopping for a whole host of facts.

Asbury's books were delightful to read, too. (Although you might be tempted to think that one or two of the facts contained therein might have been magnified a little-or a lot-for dramatic effect.) *Gangs of New York*, the book, introduced me to Gallus Mag, a six-foot-tall Englishwoman who worked at the Hole in the Wall on Wall Street. She had a reputation for biting off the ears of anyone who annoyed her, and keeping them as trophies in a jar of alcohol behind the bar. If you watch Martin Scorsese's film closely you'll spot Mag, adding an ear to the jar on the bar where Daniel Day Lewis's character, Bill the Butcher, hangs out.

## THE OBSCURE

Plugging key words such as "Prohibition," "Cocktail," and "bartender," into the search engines on antiquarian book web sites works well when researching this sort of material. But much of the information yielded has been seen in print over and over again. I wanted something new: Stories that hadn't been told for many a year; tales that might get lost if nobody re-circulated them. How would I find yarns such as these? I found that it pays to look at the bibliographies at the back of other people's books—a few hidden treasures sometimes lurk there.

From the bibliographies of various books I stumbled on *Valentine's Manual of Old New York* and *In the Golden Nineties*, books containing stories by many writers, compiled by a certain Henry Collins Brown. Within the pages of these tomes, I found information about the evolution of the ferry boat, old street names in lower Manhattan, and details of some famous Hudson River steamboats. All fascinating stuff, and well worth the time spent on the deck with a tall glass of cold pale ale, but not information that would ever make it into *The Joy of Mixology*. I was making up for all the reading I never did at school—and loving every second of it.

Brown's books did yield nuggets that I used in my book, though: information about the Old Waldorf and the Manhattan Club, for instance, came from Brown's compilations. And although I didn't use it, I still have lots of notes about the impact of the cash register on the bar business, bartenders, and bar owners, as well as other fascinating tidbits that, hopefully, will come in handy when I'm penning a future piece for some magazine or other.

Other somewhat obscure books made their way into my library by way of other folks' bibliographies, personal recommendations, yard sales, and sheer luck. All of them were dutifully read, and notes were taken when I deemed them important. Boy, did I love this work.

Consider this: I was writing a book about themes I knew well: tending bar and mixing drinks. I've been doing both those things for most of my life, and although I'm still constantly learning new stuff about both subjects, thank God, the basics are in my head. Writing *The Joy of Mixology*, for the most part, was a case of putting down on paper information that had been lurking in my grey matter for years. Researching and writing the history chapter, then, was the most rewarding part of the work. Much of the old stuff was new to me. And hopefully it was new to you, too. Which other books gave me obscure and fun facts for the chapter? You'll have to go through my bibliography and figure it out.

## FOR FURTHER READING

Asbury, Herbert. *The Gangs of New York* (New York: Thunder's Mouth Press, 2001).

Asbury, Herbert. *The Great Illusion: An Informal History of Prohibition* (New York: 1950, Doubleday & Company, Inc.).

Brown, Henry Collins, *In the Golden Nineties* (Hastings-on-Hudson: Valentine's Manual, Inc., 1928).

Brown, Henry Collins, *Valentine's Manual of Old New York* (Hastings-on-Hudson, NY: Valentine's Manual, Inc., 1927).

Sonnichsen, C. L., *Billy King's Tombstone* (Caldwell, ID: The Caxton Printers, Ltd.,1942).

# CALL FOR ENTRIES

## MIXOLOGIST

### THE JOURNAL OF THE AMERICAN COCKTAIL

Volume II • 2006

The world of Cocktails would be nothing without the persistent attention to detail of the bartenders and mixologists who create and serve these lovely libations. It takes more than a knowledge of shaking, stirring, muddling and swizzling to run a tight bar. For the featured section of the upcoming 2006 volume of *Mixologist: The Journal of the American Cocktail*, we're looking for well-researched papers on beverage operations, ranging from the process of Cocktail menu development, bar set-up and staff training, to the selection of bar equipment, glassware, bar food, spirits, liqueurs and garnishes.

For the "And Other Things" section, we welcome papers on all other subjects, from the origin of a classic Cocktail, the biography of a great bartender, a scientific study of a Cocktail ingredient or mixing technique, a recently published book on Cocktails or Cocktail history and just about anything in between.

All submissions will be subjected to a review process (read by a panel of authorities on the subjects of Cocktails and bar operations), before a decision is made on its inclusion. All writers of accepted entries will be required to sign a publication agreement.

To get a copy of the submission guidelines, visit www.mixellany.com

Send your submission as a Word document attachment to jaredbrown1@mac.com with the subject line "journal submission."

**Deadline for entries is October 1, 2005.**